REBUILDING:

IT'S NEVER TOO LATE
FOR A NEW BEGINNING

O.S. HAWKINS

Rebuilding: It's never too late for a new beginning

© 1999 O.S. Hawkins

A Publication of the Annuity Board of the Southern Baptist Convention

Unless otherwise indicated,
Scripture taken from The Believers Study Bible,
The Holy Bible, New King James Version
Copyright © 1991 by the Criswell Center for Biblical Studies

ISBN 0-9671584-0-0
BIBLE. O.T. NEHEMIAH
222.8 – dc21

Printed in the United States of America

ANNUITY BOARD
OF THE SOUTHERN
BAPTIST CONVENTION

Dedicated to

Paul May

My devoted deacon and faithful friend now in heaven.

Some people live their lives like rhythm. They simply go through life with the same old monotony, the same old beat day after day. Others are like harmony. They do their part and blend in with everyone else around them. Then, there are a few who are the melody. Paul was the melody. I feel today like Jonathon must have felt when he said to his faithful friend, David, "You will be missed because your seat will be empty" (1 Sam. 20:18). Thank you, Paul, for giving us the song for 44 beautiful and God-honoring years. I'll see you in the morning!

Table of Contents

Introduction

REBUILDING. Here is a universal subject that touches all of us as we journey through different periods of life. Many of us have relationships that need to be rebuilt. Some are in the process of rebuilding a business. I know coaches who are in the process of rebuilding their teams. Others are rebuilding integrity in their family lives. Some others are in the process of rebuilding after divorce. Some are rebuilding after the death of a loved one. Some are rebuilding their own self-confidence. Others are rebuilding their hopes for the future. Many churches are in the process of rebuilding their vision. Some persons are in the process of rebuilding their lives after retirement. In one way or the other, most all of us will spend part of the next year rebuilding. The good news is…it's never too late for a new beginning.

The more advanced we become in our techniques of rebuilding, the more we discover that the best ideas and methodologies have been proven for centuries. They simply need to be repackaged and applied to a contemporary culture. For example, a best-selling management book during the last few years was *The Leadership Secrets of Attila the Hun.* Author Wes Roberts reached into the past and brought someone to life that had been relegated to history as somewhat of a barbaric tyrant. But Attila's principles, used so long ago to motivate and mobilize his motley forces into a nation of spirited "Huns," are accurate and applicable to our world today. One might also consider the marketing success of *The Art of War* by the ancient Chinese warrior Sun Tzu. During the last decade, the strategies and management principles of this warrior philosopher of 2500 years ago have found their way into the briefcases and "war rooms" of thousands of business executives in the United States. Recently, my friend Bob Briner brought to light many of the leadership and management principles of Jesus in his best-selling books.

Now, once again from out of the past, comes a man walking down the corridors of the centuries who wrote the book on *rebuilding*. His name is Nehemiah. He was neither preacher nor prophet. He was a layman; a civil servant who applied universal principles of life that enabled him to rebuild a broken city. These principles have become the source of strength for any of us who need to rebuild today.

Nehemiah's story unfolds after the reign of King Solomon. The Kingdom of Israel was divided. The Northern Kingdom was ruled by a series of very wicked kings. In 722 B.C., the Assyrian assault led them away into captivity, from which they never returned. The Southern Kingdom was finally devastated by Babylonian supremacy in 586 B.C. The Holy City of Jerusalem was destroyed; it was virtually leveled. The temple was torn down, the walls of the city were turned to rubble, and its gates were burned. The leading Jews were taken captive into Babylon, and the Psalmist reminds us that they "hung their harps upon the willows" (Ps. 137:2). A few years later, the Persians broke up Babylonian rule and Zerubbabel returned with a remnant of people to rebuild the temple in Jerusalem. They finished the foundation, but because of the obstacles they met, quit the task after a while. Haggai and Zechariah exhorted and encouraged them to complete the work. Ezra came and reinstituted the law in Jerusalem. However, years passed, and the city was still broken down and in need of rebuilding.

Nehemiah was a Jew who had risen to prominence in the court of the Persian Emperor, Artaxerxes. This faithful layman left his civil servant job with all of his retirement benefits, returned to Jerusalem, and began the process of rebuilding the city. He has provided us with principles that unfold on the following pages. These can be applied to our lives today as we rebuild our broken walls, whether they be emotional, relational, vocational, spiritual, or whatever. As we examine his memoirs in the Old Testament, we too will discover...*it's never too late for a new beginning.*

Part I

Rebuilders get started right

Rebuilders get started right. I enjoy playing golf. The most important shot in golf is the tee shot. Every hole is a new beginning. At each hole, you step up on the tee and hit your first shot, which generally determines how well you will do on the hole. If you drive the ball in the woods, you have to "scramble" with two or three other shots in order to get to the green. If you drive the ball out of bounds you are penalized an additional shot. However, if you drive the ball straight down the fairway and position yourself for the second shot to the green, you are well on your way to finishing the hole strongly.

Many never score well in golf because they spend most of their time trying to make up yardage lost by poor tee shots. Getting started right is essential, whether we are playing golf or rebuilding.

There is a very real sense in which rebuilding something is far more difficult than building something from scratch. During my days in the pastorate, I was privileged to pastor two of the greatest churches in America, the First Baptist Church in Fort Lauderdale, Florida, and the First Baptist Church in Dallas, Texas. The challenge in Fort Lauderdale was to build a myriad of ministries without a lot of traditional history behind us. In Dallas, the task was to rebuild upon the great foundation of two pastors who led the church for 100 years.

When we are in the process of rebuilding, there are not just things that need to be *done*; there are also things that need to be *undone*. There are habits that need to be broken...sometimes there are hearts that need to be healed. Anyone who has ever rebuilt a marriage or a church knows this. This is why for some people it's easier to start over than to pay the price of rebuilding. Whether we are rebuilding our lives, our marriage, our church, our business, or any number of other issues, the challenge for us all is to *get started right* in the process of rebuilding.

Are you in need of *rebuilding* something? Does it seem as though you simply cannot get started right? Nehemiah is here to show us in Chapter One *how to get started right*. For almost a century, others had seen the need to rebuild those broken walls of Jerusalem. Some had even tried. Then, Nehemiah came on the scene and accomplished the task in less than two months. How did he do it? He outlines in Chapter One of his book some principles that will enable us *to get started right*. He shows us that rebuilders make an honest evaluation. They identify with the need. They take personal responsibility. And, they move out of their comfort zones.

The most difficult and challenging part of any journey is the beginning...*getting started right*. This is true whether we are on a journey of dieting, or exercising, or attempting to rebuild a broken relationship. Nehemiah begins with the importance of getting started right and the rest of his book relates an unfolding of principles which, when applied, see us to the accomplishment of our task. Yes, *rebuilders get started right, and when they do, they discover…it's never too late for a new beginning!*

Chapter One

Make an honest evaluation

NEHEMIAH opens his memoirs with the news of a report from distant Jerusalem. Someone had returned from a visit, and Nehemiah inquired concerning not only the Jews, but the condition of the Holy City itself. The report was, "The survivors who are left from the captivity in the province are there in great distress and reproach. The wall of Jerusalem is also broken down, and its gates are burned with fire" (Neh. 1:3).

If Nehemiah was to get started right in being the agent of rebuilding, his first step now was to *make an honest evaluation* of the condition in Jerusalem. Although a remnant of the Jews had returned home and the temple was in place, there was only a semblance of normalcy. The walls of the city were broken down, and its gates were still burned with fire. The people who returned had become a reproach by their own lifestyles. They were "in distress." They were "a reproach." When we do not finish the job God gives us to do, it becomes a reproach and leads others to exclaim, "some God you must have!"

Nehemiah's evaluation also saw that the walls were

broken down. They were in dire need of being rebuilt in order to provide security and safety for the inhabitants of Jerusalem. And as though that were not enough, the gates of the city were burned with fire; thus, they were vulnerable to the enemy.

Nehemiah saw his city for what it was. *He made an honest evaluation.* Many of us never rebuild because we don't make an honest evaluation of our own circumstances and situations. We never admit our need. We never confess that some of our own walls are broken and some of our own gates are burned. The sensing of our pain, as agonizing as it may be, often begins the healing process. People have met premature deaths because they will not face the warning signs of pain. Some will not go to their personal physicians for an honest evaluation of physical needs. The same can be said of relationships or any other thing that is in need of rebuilding. *To get started right,* the first step is to pause and *make an honest evaluation of our lives.*

There are at least three ways to begin to rebuild that which is broken. One is the way of a superficial optimist. This is the cosmetic approach that deals only with surface issues and is in the constant process of trying to put a positive spin on a difficult situation. The superficial optimist usually resists making an honest evaluation, thinking if you just wait long enough, and hunker down far enough, everything will go away. The ancient prophet, Jeremiah, dealt with such leaders when he said, "Saying 'Peace, peace!' When there is no peace" (Jer. 8:11).

There are others who approach the rebuilding process as realists. That is, they admit the problem, but approach it by trying to get everyone around them as busy as they possibly can. They set up new organizations. They put together a new crew. They develop new courses. But new crews and new courses will not keep the ship afloat if there is a hole in the hull.

There are others who make honest evaluations and then have the courage to face the root problems honestly. They have the wisdom and understanding, as well as the strength and patience, to do something. And they have the faith to trust God to work through the circumstance and situation. Those who make honest evaluations are not afraid of losing friends or making enemies. They are not intimidated by threats, and they are not for sale. Such a man was Nehemiah. He got started right by making an honest evaluation.

There are many of us in need of rebuilding today. Perhaps some readers have taken the superficial optimist approach, simply dealing with surface issues and all the while crying, "Peace, peace," when there really is no peace. Perhaps there are others who more closely identify with the realist approach; instead of rebuilding you simply move on to new people or new projects. But learn from Nehemiah. Look at him. He is making an honest evaluation. He inquires, and then admits that not only are the walls broken down and the gates burned, but also the people are in distress and have become a reproach.

Are there any unfinished projects in your life? Any walls that need rebuilding? Those who win in life always finish what they start, but before that ever happens, they get started right by making an honest evaluation. Rebuilders who go through the painful process of making honest evaluations are soon on the road to the realization that...*it's never too late for a new beginning.*

Chapter Two

Identify with the need

WHEN Nehemiah heard the report from Jerusalem and made an honest evaluation, his passion index rose. His next impulse was to identify with the need. He continues, "So it was, when I heard these words, that I sat down and wept, and mourned for many days; I was fasting and praying before the God of heaven" (Neh. 1:4).

Nehemiah not only cared enough to make inquiry and an honest evaluation, he cared enough to identify with the need. He sat down. He put everything else aside and contemplated the matter. As he did so, he "sat down and wept." He thought about the reproach and the distress, the broken walls and burned gates, and tears welled up in his eyes and ran down his cheeks. The more I have personally studied the process of rebuilding, the more I have become convinced that one never rebuilds until he or she weeps over the ruins. We have a contemporary culture that is losing its tears today. In a day when contemporary Christianity is filled with wealth and happiness, with cults whose primary motives are personal enjoyment, we do not hear very much about this kind of passion. When Nehemiah heard the report from Jerusalem, his passion index rose!

Nehemiah's concern was not simply the welfare of the people, but also the glory of God. For him, prayer was warfare. He agonized; he wept; he mourned; he fasted for days. Is it any wonder God used him to rebuild the broken walls of Jerusalem? He not only made an honest evaluation, he truly identified with the need. He did what all leaders must do...he drew his strength from outside himself. He identified with those in need, and he lived with this burden for four months.

What about your passion index? Rate your passion index for rebuilding on a scale of one to ten, with ten being a burning desire, and one being simply a heap of ashes. If your passion for your own project is lower than a seven, you will probably never see the task of rebuilding accomplished. In fact, the whole process of rebuilding will simply become another burden to you, and you will find yourself in frustration and going through the motions. Those who rebuild begin to circle themselves with people who have a burning passion for what God has led them and called them to do. They identify with the needs around them.

Tragically, some of us are simply not very grieved or burdened about the walls around our lives that need to be rebuilt. How long has it been since those of us in need of rebuilding something have sat down? How long has it been since we have wept? Or mourned? Or fasted? Or prayed for days and months? Rebuilders get started right, and the only way to do this is to make a proper evaluation, and identify with the needs around you. In so doing, Nehemiah brought his people to a sense of camaraderie. He was, by his own example of leadership, illustrating to them that...*it's never too late for a new beginning.*

Chapter Three

Take personal responsibility

NEHEMIAH could have faced his dilemma by blaming all his current problems on his past difficulties. That is, if Nebuchadnezzar had simply not besieged the city of Jerusalem and taken the Jews captive, the need of rebuilding would have never been known. Or, if they simply had not been taken into battle, they could have gotten on with the project much more quickly. Perhaps if Zerubbabel had been more zealous about the task of rebuilding at the very beginning of the return of the remnant, things would have been different. Yes, Nehemiah could have blamed all his current problems on past difficulties. He could have pointed fingers of accusation at Jehoiachin, Zedekiah, and the other kings of Judah. They betrayed their people. No wonder the walls were broken. There were plenty of people who could have been blamed, but those who play the "blame game" never get the rebuilding job done. We now see Nehemiah refusing to point fingers of accusation in other people's directions, but instead taking personal responsibility for the dilemma himself. This is a characteristic that generally follows those who make honest evaluations and identify with the needs.

There are many churches that fall to the temptations of blaming all their present problems on past people. Falling into this trap keeps one from moving forward. Nehemiah could have blamed others, but he did not. His ultimate goal was getting those walls rebuilt, so he was focused on the importance of getting started right.

Listen to him as he prays and confesses the sins of the children of Israel, "...which we have sinned against You. Both my father's house and I have sinned. We have acted very corruptly against You" (Neh. 1:6-7). Note the plural pronouns. He is saying *"we,"* not *"they."* True rebuilders identify with the failures and fears of the people around them. They not only identify with the need, they take personal responsibility themselves. Nehemiah is team-building early on in the process. It is easy to see what he is doing. He is confessing other people's sins as though they were his very own. Leaders identify with the need and take personal responsibility with their people. Note that he did not say "they made a mistake," nor did he say "if" we have sinned. Nehemiah was crying out to God with plural pronouns *"we,"* and personal pronouns *"I."*

Perhaps it is this very point more than anything else that keeps men and women from being rebuilders. Often we are too intent on blaming everyone else for our broken walls and burned gates. For many, it is always someone else's fault. This is why many relationships are never rebuilt. This is why many homes are broken. This is the very reason some churches do not live together in love and unity. It never dawns upon some of us to take personal responsibility. Unfortunately, we are too busy trying to place blame on others, often seeking to justify our own innocence in the process. The task of rebuilding will never be accomplished until we take personal responsibility.

What is interesting to me is that it only takes one person to initiate the process of rebuilding. Nehemiah was one man, but what a difference he made when he got started right. He did what everyone of us who need to rebuild something around us should be doing. He made an honest evaluation of his circumstance and situation. There was no glossing over the circumstance. There was no covering over the issue. Next, he identified with the need. He felt it; it became the prayer burden of his heart. Then he took personal responsibility. He identified with his people.

It only takes one person to get the rebuilding process started, whether it is in the home, in the office, in the church, or in the social arena. One person can make a huge difference. Just look at Nehemiah...*it's never too late for a new beginning.*

Chapter Four

Move out of your comfort zone

NEHEMIAH concludes the first chapter of his memoirs with a simple sentence: "For I was the king's cupbearer" (Neh. 1:11). On the surface, this certainly does not sound too impressive. What was he? Dishwasher? Waiter? A type of bus boy? What is he saying in this simple statement that seems to be out of context and simply an addendum to the chapter? There is so much behind these words. Nehemiah is relating to us the truth; he was, in fact, the king's trusted confidant. He was the king's cupbearer. He tasted the king's drink and food before the king. He was constantly by his side. He was a faithful counsel to the most important man in the land. His position gives us a bit of insight into Nehemiah's character and reputation. The king of Persia, the world power of its day, would only select the wisest, most honest, loyal, and trustworthy person he could find to be his cupbearer. The point is simply this – Nehemiah had it made. He was fixed for life. He had a civil service job with incredible retirement benefits. He was a man who moved out of his comfort zone, and was paying the price to be the agent of rebuilding.

Many of us live in a culture not only out in the world, but within the church, that is asking, "What is in it for me?" When many young families are looking for churches today, their first question is, "What can you do for me?" In our contemporary culture, many look for a church home where they do not have to be inconvenienced. Very few people are ready to move out of their comfort zones, and consequently there is not enough rebuilding being done today.

I grew up in Texas. Most boys in Texas grow up living for football season in the fall. What is the one common characteristic of all the great professional football teams throughout the modern era? Every major football dynasty has one person who is extremely proficient in passing the ball. The Green Bay Packers had their Bart Starr. The Dallas Cowboys have their Don Meredith, Roger Staubach, and Troy Aikman. The Pittsburgh Steelers had Terry Bradshaw. The San Francisco 49ers had Joe Montana and Steve Young. Throwing the forward pass in football is risky business. It moves us out of our comfort zone. Darrell Royal, the legendary coach of the University of Texas, said there were four things that may happen when you throw a pass, and three of them are bad. The good thing that can happen is that you complete the pass. The bad things are that the quarterback can be sacked, the pass can be thrown incomplete and the down lost, or the other team could intercept the pass.

Years ago, there was a time when football teams had difficulty moving out of their comfort zone. The year was 1905. Most of the games played on the college gridiron were low-scoring games characterized by running and kicking. There were guys in leather helmets running in the flying wedge. There were three yards and a cloud of dust. It was a tough, dirty, gritty game that was "played between the tackles." In 1906, the forward pass was legalized, making it possible to gain as much as forty yards with the flick of a wrist. However, during that first season, teams stayed within their comfort zones. They kept running. They kept doing what they had always done. They kept doing what was comfortable. Realizing a new day had come, St. Louis University moved out of its comfort zone. That first year they switched almost entirely to the forward pass, and that season outscored their opponents 402-11. The rest is history.

Today, the church of Jesus Christ, moving into the third millennium, faces changes as challenging as the introduction of the forward pass to football. We are called to reach a post-modern world in what is a post-Christian culture. Many are scrambling. Many are trying to win without any innovations. The result is they stay in their comfort zones and are defeated and left behind.

The world our churches need to reach today is not the world of "Ozzie and Harriet" or "The Beaver." We are trying to reach a contemporary culture where everyone is not living in a tidy little home behind a white picket fence with nothing to do except attend religious services. We are called to reach men and women all around us with a tremendous need to rebuild lives.

Rebuilding means that we must move out of our comfort zones. This is exactly what our Lord Jesus Christ did when He walked the roads of this world. He was constantly engaged with moving us out of our comfort zones. If we are ever going to begin the process of rebuilding in our own personal experiences, we must follow His lead.

Nehemiah says, "I was the cupbearer to the King." "So

what?" you may ask. For Nehemiah, it meant leaving the comfort zone. It meant taking a risk. It meant returning to Jerusalem. It meant becoming vulnerable. But the result was wonderful. He became the agent of an incredible process of rebuilding which brought much good to others, and much glory to God.

Are there any walls in your life in need of repair? Are there any gates that once protected you that are now burned down? Are there walls that once were strong but now have cracks in the mortar? Perhaps a stone slipped loose here, and another there, and some parts of your wall began to weaken and cave in. The Lord Jesus Christ came to be the rebuilder of our own broken walls. He said to us through the prophet Isaiah, "Can a woman forget her nursing child, and not have compassion on the son of her womb? Surely they may forget, yet I will not forget you. See, I have inscribed you on the palms of My hands; your walls are continually before Me" (Is. 49:15-16).

Our Lord saw each of our lives broken. What did he do? He came to be our rebuilder. He got started right. He made an honest evaluation. Then he identified with the need. He came and wept over the city of Jerusalem. Next, he took personal responsibility. He took our sin in His own body. He died our death so we could live His life. He took upon Himself the iniquities of us all. And, he moved out of His comfort zone. He laid aside His glory and clothed Himself in human flesh. Why? So you and I could have a new beginning.

Getting started right is the most important step in the rebuilding process. Some who plan on rebuilding have just never gotten started. Make an honest evaluation. Identify with the need. Take personal responsibility. And, move out of your comfort zone. When you do, you will get started right and you too will discover that...*it's never too late for a new beginning.*

Part II

Rebuilders build a team spirit

NEHEMIAH is proving to be a wise sage when it comes to the process of rebuilding. We have seen that in one way or another we are all in this process. In many ways, rebuilding is a much more difficult task than building something from scratch. There are not just things that need to be *done*, in the rebuilding process, there are also things that need to be *undone*! Often there are habits that need to be broken and attitudes that need to be changed. Sometimes there are hurts that need to be healed. Anyone who has ever rebuilt a life after a broken marriage knows this to be true. Rebuilding is a challenge, but it is also an exciting and rewarding adventure.

We have seen that rebuilders get started right. Beginnings are vitally important. In fact, I doubt that anyone has seen the rebuilding process through to completion that did not get started right. He or she made an honest evaluation of the circumstance, identified with the need, took personal responsibility, and moved out of the comfort zone.

As we continue through Nehemiah's memoirs, we now learn a second important lesson in rebuilding. *Rebuilders build a team spirit.* They say "we" a lot. This truth echoes throughout the verses of Nehemiah's experience in Chapter Two of the book that bears his name. He is building team spirit. As we rebuild, it is essential to get those around us to be part of our team and to follow our leadership. It is a team sport, whether we are rebuilding a life, a business, a church, a marriage, or whatever.

The most successful athletic franchises are those who play as a team. 1998 was one of the great years in Major League Baseball history. Throughout most of the year, the spotlight shone on two individuals, Mark McGwire and Sammy Sosa. They were involved in a nail-biting homerun race that eventually saw McGwire break the all-time record for homeruns in a season. However, neither of their teams won the big prize. The New York Yankees, setting a record for most wins in a season, won the World Series. They did it without one major superstar rising above the others. They played together as a team. It was one for all, and all for one, and they are the ones who wound up on top. Experience has proven that the most successful homes are those who play as a team. The most successful businesses are those who build a team spirit. The most successful churches are those who live and love together as a team. Getting started right is essential, but building a team spirit is what keeps the rebuilding process in motion.

How does one build a team spirit? Nehemiah shows us the way in Chapter Two of his memoirs as he outlines five steps for us to follow. He reminds us in Nehemiah 2:1-5 that if we are ever going to rebuild we must start with our goal in mind. People want to know where we are taking them and how we plan to get there. Before Nehemiah left Persia, before he recruited the first person in Jerusalem, before he motivated his people, before he removed the rubbish of the broken down walls, he started with his goal in mind.

Next, he reminds us to seize our opportunities (Neh. 2:4-10). Hear him as he beseeches the king to "send me" (Neh. 2:5). Here was a man who seized his opportunities and moved out of his comfort zone. Then he calls us to make a careful analysis of our situation (Neh. 2:11-16). That is, take a good and careful and honest look at the ruins that need to be rebuilt around our lives. Next, he challenges us to motivate our people to get off dead center (Neh. 2:17-18). Finally, in order to build a team spirit, Nehemiah speaks of the importance of staying on track (Neh. 2:19-20). If the rebuilding process is to be completed and team building is to be accomplished, we must not let anyone or anything divert us or get us off track. Rebuilders keep focused. They build a team spirit because they are convinced...*it's never too late for a new beginning.*

Chapter 5

Start with your goal in mind

BEFORE Nehemiah ever laid a stone in the rebuilding process, before he ever recruited a worker, before he ever left Persia, he lived with a burden and *started with his goal in mind*. He knew where he was going, and he knew how he was going to get there. The king himself noticed his burden and asked, "Why is your face sad, since you are not sick? This is nothing but sorrow of heart" (Neh. 2:2). Nehemiah had been carrying this burden for four months, since he had first heard the report of the broken down walls and the burned gates. His reply to the king biblically illustrates that his goal was in mind long before he set out for Jerusalem. He says, "Why should my face not be sad, when the city, the place of my fathers' tombs, lies waste, and its gates are burned with fire?" (Neh. 2:3). He had a passion for what God had put in his heart…to rebuild Jerusalem! Nehemiah laid bare his heart, and the king read him like a book. Here is a man who's living with a goal in mind.

Anyone who's ever accomplished the process of rebuilding in life knows where they're going and how they're going to get there. In our sports-crazed Western world, the most recognized face and name is Michael Jordan. Words are useless to attempt to describe his athletic prowess on the basketball court as he played for the Chicago Bulls. After 15 years of playing in the National Basketball Association, Michael Jordan averaged 32 points a game during that entire span of years. It didn't matter who the Chicago Bulls were playing, who was guarding him, or what injuries he may have been nursing, he managed to get 32 points a game. Some time ago, a reporter asked him how he was able to maintain this average for all those years. Michael Jordan replied, "I simplify the matter. It takes only eight points per quarter to score 32 points a game. I find some way each quarter to simply get those eight points." What is Michael Jordan saying? He is saying that he starts each game with a goal in mind. He knows where he is going and how he is going to get there before the opening tip-off even occurs. Those in the process of rebuilding could learn a lesson from Nehemiah and Michael Jordan, and see the importance of starting with your goal in mind, particularly if you are interested in building team spirit.

As we read these verses from Nehemiah Chapter Two, it is apparent what he had in mind. What was his goal? To rebuild the walls of Jerusalem. He knew where he was going and how he was going to get there. Later in his book, we will see hundreds and hundreds of people following his leadership as the walls are being rebuilt. Why? Because Nehemiah built a team spirit and he began by starting with his goal in mind.

There are many homes in trouble today because men and women do not know where they are going. They have no goal in mind, with family goals that are broken down by "quarters." Thus, there is no direction or purpose. The Bible clearly delineates goals for the home in Ephesians 5. The husband is the key in loving his wife sacrificially and selflessly, as Christ loved the church. It is easy to respond in loving mutual submission to that kind of love, because it always has your highest goal in mind.

The reason many churches in America are stagnant or dying is because there is no team spirit. Why? It is at this very point...they have no goal in mind and do not know where they are going, much less how they are going to get there. The Lord Jesus Christ has given the goal of the church in explicit terms in the New Testament. We are to fulfill the Great Commission and the Great Commandment. It is the church's task to share the gospel of Christ with everyone, baptize them into the family of faith, and teach them to grow to maturity. The church is also to love the Lord supremely and our neighbors as ourselves.

Is anyone reading these words that is in need of rebuilding something in your life? Rebuilding is a team sport, and we begin playing as a team when we start with our goal in mind. Rebuilders not only get started right, they build a team spirit by knowing where they are going and how they are going to get there. Therefore, they know...*it's never too late for a new beginning.*

Chapter Six

Seize your opportunities

In Nehemiah Chapter Two, we find Nehemiah standing before King Artaxerxes, who asked a pointed question, "What do you request?" Nehemiah seized his opportunity and said, "…send me to Judah, to the city of my fathers' tombs, that I may rebuild it" (Neh. 2:5). Carpe Diem! He seized the day. He took advantage of his opportunity. The king then asked three more questions, "What do you request?" (Neh. 2:4), "How long will your journey be? And when will you return?" (Neh. 2:6). Nehemiah had been praying and planning for four months, and now he seized his opportunities. He had thought it through, and had all the right answers for the king. He even knew that Asaph, the king's forester, could furnish the needed materials. And he was cautious to give God all the credit (Neh. 2:8).

How many opportunities to rebuild come our way and pass us by because we never seize our opportunities? We are what we are in part because of what we do with opportunities that come our way. For some time now, Nehemiah had prayed and planned and prepared. When the door cracked open, he seized his opportunity and requested to be sent back to Judah to become the agent of rebuilding. Tragically, some of us never rebuild, even though we may get started right. We begin to build team spirit with a goal in mind, but never seize our opportunities when they come. Perhaps God is asking you today, "what do you want?" or, "what do you need?" He is saying to you... *it's never too late for a new beginning.*

Chapter Seven

Make a careful analysis of your situation

BEFORE the rebuilding process in Jerusalem had begun or a single person had been recruited and motivated for the task, Nehemiah made a careful analysis of his situation. When he came to Jerusalem, he waited for three days, and in the middle of the night made a midnight ride to survey the ruined walls. "I told no one what my God had put in my heart to do at Jerusalem" (Neh. 2:12). Nehemiah made a careful analysis of the situation.

Leadership can be lonely. Before any major work of rebuilding, someone must take a midnight ride and make a careful analysis of the situation, and perhaps, like Nehemiah, even weep over the ruins. He did not send someone to check it out for him. There are some things that simply cannot be delegated. Those who lead others to accomplish great tasks usually struggle long and hard and alone before their plans are ever made public. They, like Nehemiah, saddle up and take a late-night ride to review the ruins. In building a team spirit, they make a careful analysis of their situation.

Those who get the job of rebuilding done do not rush in before they do their homework. They take a good long look at the situation for themselves. It is part of the price of leadership. Some do not accomplish rebuilding not necessarily because they do not start with a goal in mind or seize their opportunities. It is due to the fact that they fail to make a careful and detailed analysis of the situation as it really is.

Nehemiah's midnight journey was not simply a casual glance at the ruins. The Bible tells us that he "viewed" the broken down walls (Neh. 2:13-15). The Hebrew word which we translate "viewed" into our English Bibles is actually a medical term that describes a physician "who looks into a wound very carefully." The word describes a doctor who "probes the wound to fully examine it." This was no casual glance at some broken down stones. It was a careful analysis of the situation.

My first pastorate was in the wheat farming country of southwestern Oklahoma in the small town of Hobart. On rare occasions, a few of the oldtimers would make a request that the pastor be in the operating room when they were having surgery. As a young pastor, I would "scrub up" with the local surgeon and be present in the operating room for prayer during the surgery. It was an amazing education for me! In biology classes, I had seen diagrams of the human organs that appeared to be so neatly in place within our abdomens. Not true! I would watch that skilled surgeon probe all of the vital organs in an exploratory abdominal surgery. He would lift them in his hands, examine them, and thoroughly "view" those organs that were vital to the person's well-being. This is the same word that Nehemiah used to describe what he did that evening as he took his midnight ride to "view" the walls of Jerusalem. He made a careful analysis of the situation.

Nehemiah viewed all of the debris that had been piled up for years. There was accumulated trash around the walls of Jerusalem, and nothing had been done to remove it. I've seen this happen in many lives. I've seen it happen in marriages, in businesses, even in churches. There are things that begin to pile up over the years and get in the way of healthy and wholesome relationships, and often nothing is done. Rebuilding demands that we have the courage to make a careful analysis of our situation.

Rebuilders build a team spirit. How? They get people on their team by starting with their goal in mind, by seizing their opportunities, and by making a careful analysis of their situation. Perhaps there are attitudes, actions, or other debris that have piled up in our lives over the years and have gotten in the way of the rebuilding process. Rebuilders have one thing in common...they know *it's never too late for a new beginning.*

Chapter Eight

Motivate your people to get off dead center

WHEN we come to Chapter Three of the book of Nehemiah, we see that the actual rebuilding process begins. However, before it does, we find in Chapter Two that Nehemiah is building a team spirit with his people. He encourages them to get off dead center. He is able to motivate them to adopt his goal because he followed three important lessons in goal setting. (1) He made sure that his goal of rebuilding was conceivable. That is, he wanted to know that others could easily conceive of the task ahead. He wanted them to understand what needed to be done. (2) He made sure his goal of rebuilding was believable. He had some goals people could believe in. He was dealing with men and women who had been living in discouragement for years who needed to believe again. Hear him as he challenges them in Nehemiah 2: 17-18 saying, "Let's do it; we can do it. The hand of our God is with us." The people not only conceived the goal, they began to believe it. (3) Then Nehemiah made sure that his goal was achievable. This goal was not outside their reach. They could do it. If they could rebuild the temple, they could rebuild the walls and the gates.

Here is some wonderful practical advice from one of the greatest motivators of men and women and one of the most effective rebuilders the world has ever known. Can you see what he is doing? Nehemiah is building a team spirit. How? He has started with his goal in mind; he has seized his opportunities; he has made a careful analysis of his situation; and now he's beginning to motivate his people to get off dead center.

If every church could get people to see the dynamic of Nehemiah 2:17-18, they would impact their neighborhoods and beyond them, their worlds. In these verses Nehemiah said to them, "'You see the distress that we are in, how Jerusalem lies waste, and its gates are burned with fire. Come and let us build the wall of Jerusalem, that we may no longer be a reproach.' And I told them of the hand of my God which had been good upon me, and also of the king's words that he had spoken to me. So they said, 'Let us rise up and build.' Then they set their hands to this good work" (Neh. 2:17-18). Nehemiah motivates his people to get off dead center. How? He led them to do four things in building this team spirit. He led them to face up, team up, gird up, and look up.

First, Nehemiah led his people to "face up". He said to them, "You see the distress that we are in, how Jerusalem lies waste…?" (Neh. 2:17). He's calling upon them to wake up, to face up, and open their eyes. They had been looking, but now he wanted them to see. For years they had been looking at that wall. They had gotten used to it. Others had come to Jerusalem and seen it as a reproach, but they were blind to it. We will never rebuild our individual lives until we, too, face up. This is true whether we are trying to rebuild a marriage, a life, a business, a church, or whatever. It is ironic, but it often takes someone new to get us to see things that are right under our noses. Years of familiarity have a way of causing us to look at things without really seeing them. This is exactly why the wise counsel of Christian friends is so valuable. Quite often, it takes someone new, like Nehemiah, to get us to face up to our own needs around us. We will never be motivated to complete our task until we "face up."

Next, Nehemiah called upon his people to "team up." There are three very important words he uses in Nehemiah 2:17: "we," "us," "we." Nehemiah uses plural pronouns a lot. Do you see what he is doing? He is challenging his people to work *with him*, not *for him*. What kind of response do you think he would have had from these people had he approached it by saying, "You people are unbelievable. You've been here all these years, and look at you. What have you been doing? You have gotten yourself into a pitiful position. You know what you need to do. You need to rebuild the walls. Why haven't you done it? I am not the problem. I just got here. Now, get on with the task." He could have berated them with second person pronouns: "you," "you," "you." Playing the blame game with constant criticism will squelch motivation. Listen to what Nehemiah is saying by using these plural pronouns. He is saying, "Team up."

Some never rebuild because it's always a matter of "you," "you," "you." We are often quick to have the attitude that says, "You see the mess you are in. You made your own bed. You'd better get your act together." How many parents have said that to their children and squelched any motivation they may have had? How much better the result might have been had we said "we" more than "you." How many husband-wife relationships might have been rebuilt had we faced up and teamed up? How many pastors have never really rebuilt because they used their pulpit to berate and bully, instead of building team spirit? Rebuilders use "we" a lot. They know that unless they build a team spirit, they will never see the rebuilding process completed.

California anthropologist, Angeles Arrien, draws some very important corporate and business principles from the study of migrating geese. We have all seen them flying in their "V" formation. What can we learn about building team spirit, about facing up, and teaming up from a bunch of geese? (1) Each bird flaps his wings and creates an uplift for the birds behind. A bird has 71% more flying range in a "V" formation than he does by flying alone. The lesson is obvious. When we share a common purpose and direction, we can all get there quicker and with much less effort. (2) Whenever a goose gets out of formation, he immediately feels resistance in trying to go it alone, and gets back into the formation with the others. Again, the lesson should be pretty obvious. If we had as much sense as a goose, we would stay in formation with those who are going the same way we are. It's much harder to get the job done when we are always flying alone. (3) When the lead goose gets tired, he rotates back into the formation and another goose flies on the point. The lesson? We all need each other, and everyone should share the harder jobs so we can all reach our goal together. Also, the geese in the formation honk from behind to encourage those in front to keep up their speed. If you happen to be fortunate enough to see them flying over, you will hear them honking to one another. The lesson is, when we honk at those in the lead, we should make sure we are honking words of encouragement and not words of discouragement. (4) When one of the geese is sick or wounded and falls out of the formation to the ground, two others fall out and follow the wounded goose, staying with it until it either revives or dies. What a lesson! If men and women knew we stood together like that in the church of the Lord Jesus Christ, there would be more people on our team and sharing our vision. Nehemiah is building a team spirit. How? He is motivating his people to get off dead center by causing them to face up and team up.

Nehemiah also calls upon his people to "gird up." Listen to him as he says, "Come and let us build the wall of Jerusalem..." (Neh. 2:17). It is impossible to get people to gird up if they don't first face up and team up. These people were not following Nehemiah. They were following his vision! People do not give themselves to needs; they give themselves to visions. These people had seen the need for years and had done nothing about it. When a dad gets a vision for his home, it's easy for the other team members to get on board. The same is true in the office, in the church, or wherever we may be.

It is interesting to note here that Nehemiah called his people to do something tangible. He said, "Let's build the walls." He had a burden, but he didn't motivate men and women by saying, "Let's arise and get a burden like mine." Also, he did not focus on the miserable state they were in. We do not motivate people to get off dead center by causing them to look backward, but by causing them to look forward. People are in need of a leader. Why? Because so many are discouraged. We never lead others by discouragement. Nehemiah lived with a burden for four months, but he did not try to motivate people out of sympathy. What leads men and women to accomplish their goals? It is optimism. It is that "can do" spirit. Listen to Nehemiah, "We are going to do it!" "Let's get up and go for it!" "Let's do it together!" "We can do it!"

Finally, Nehemiah motivates his people to get off dead center, not simply by facing up, teaming up, and girding up, but he challenges them to "look up." He says, "I told them of the hand of my God which had been good upon me" (Neh. 2:18). He convinced his people that the hand of God was upon them. People have a way of rallying around something when they see God is in it! Now, what was Nehemiah's motive? Was it to have the biggest wall in that part of the world? Was it to have more men and women than anywhere gather on that wall? What was Nehemiah's motive? He explicitly reveals it in Nehemiah 2:17: "…that we may no longer be a reproach." He is saying, "Look up! God is with us!" Nehemiah's primary concern was for the glory of God.

Now, let's make some application. Take a marriage, for example. How can we get off dead center in a marriage relationship and see it rebuilt for the glory of God? The first step is to "face up." Some of us have been looking at our broken walls for years without taking any personal responsibility and admitting the "distress" we are in. Once you face up, then you can "team up." You cannot rebuild alone. There is a synergy that comes when two are together. Then, quite honestly, there is a time to "gird up". Marriage is hard work and it takes a "can do" attitude of those who will "put their hands to the plow and not look back." Finally, it is necessary to "look up." The truth is, we all need help outside ourselves. We all need to acknowledge that the hand of our God is good upon us, and our ultimate purpose is to bring Him glory.

These same four steps are motivational influences, no

matter what we are seeking to rebuild. Those who are rebuilding after divorce, or even after the death of a spouse, can take the same route. That is, face up; stop blaming others and deal with the reality at hand. Team up; realize that we need each other. Gird up; get out of bed, and begin to work on the problems at hand. Accept the fact that life goes on and certain things must be done. Look up, and know that it is, in fact, never too late for a new beginning with God. We have an advantage as Christians. Others face up, team up, and gird up, but we are the only ones who can also "look up."

Do you see what is happening here? We are seeing a vision birthed and adopted in Nehemiah Chapter Two. These men and women were motivated to get off dead center because their leader had a vision. He had started with his goal in mind, seized his opportunities, made a careful analysis of his situation, and now he motivates his people to get on his team with him.

The birth and maturity of a vision is like the birth of a baby. It involves several stages. There is the stage of conception. This takes place when the seed of man and the egg of woman come together and the baby is conceived. Nehemiah's vision was conceived in Nehemiah 1:3-4. Next comes the stage of gestation. This is when, for months, the baby grows within the womb of the mother. For four months, Nehemiah gestated the vision God had given him (Neh. 2:12). Then comes birth. The baby is born! Nehemiah birthed his vision in Nehemiah 2:17. Here he let it out for all to see. This is followed by the stage of adoption, one of the most beautiful words in the English language. This is when two people adopt as their very own a child they haven't physically conceived, gestated, or birthed. However, by all rights, that child becomes their very own. This is what Nehemiah saw happen in Nehemiah 2:18. The Bible says, "So they said, 'Let us rise up and build.' Then they set their hands to this good work."

The next stage in the development of a child is growth. This is when the child begins to grow through the stages and seasons of life. We will see in Nehemiah Chapter Three that the wall is going up. However, like a child, its growth is not without challenges. Then comes the stage of maturity, when everything we have dreamed of and hoped for in our child comes to maturity. For me, that took place not long ago when I walked my daughter down an aisle and put her hand in the hand of a handsome young man that God had chosen for her. Nehemiah's vision becomes mature in Nehemiah 6:15 when the Bible records that "...the wall was finished." After this, there comes the important stage of reproduction. There are many churches and individuals who see all of their vision reach maturity, but never dream again, never reproduce their vision again, and continue to live in mediocrity. In the following chapters after the wall was completed, Nehemiah begins to lead in the rebuilding of a nation. He challenges Judah to dream new dreams and have bigger visions.

When Nehemiah gave his challenge in Nehemiah 2:17-18, the people's negative feelings turned to positive. Discouragement gave way to hope. They had something to look forward to, a goal in mind. A team spirit emerged. They had gotten off dead center.

It only takes one person with a God-given vision in the home, or the office, or church, or wherever, to make a difference. Often it takes someone new, like Nehemiah, to help us "see," instead of simply "look." Nehemiah was rebuilding. How? He had gotten started right, and now he's building a team spirit. He has motivated his people to get off dead center. He has said to them, and now to us, "Face up, team up, gird up, and look up, because... *it's never too late for a new beginning.*"

Chapter Nine

Stay on track

NEHEMIAH was successful in part because of one word... *focus!* He stayed on track. However, there will always be those who try to get us sidetracked. This is shown in Nehemiah through the verses which record, "But when Sanballat the Horonite, Tobiah the Ammonite official, and Gesham the Arab heard of it, they laughed at us and despised us, and said, 'What is this thing that you are doing? Will you rebel against the king?' So I answered them, and said to them, 'The God of heaven Himself will prosper us; therefore we His servants will arise and build, but you have no heritage or right or memorial in Jerusalem.'" (Neh. 2:19-20).

Here we see the origin of a group of negative individuals who did their best to divert Nehemiah from his goal. They begin here in Chapter Two, and they do not let up throughout the whole process of rebuilding. Their attempt to get Nehemiah sidetracked is continuous. It is revealed in Nehemiah 2:10, 19; 4:1-3, 7-8; 6:1-2. Nehemiah's target was clearly defined. So, like a fighter pilot, he locked in on his goal of rebuilding the walls of Jerusalem, and focused on staying on track. Those who are rebuilders recognize that they cannot, and will not, please everyone. Quite honestly, some folks are comfortable in their own ruins. It is often a fact that as soon as someone comes along with God's vision of rebuilding there will always be someone else to oppose it.

Staying on track is vitally important. I lived in Fort Lauderdale for 15 years, and always enjoyed the time of spring training for the baseball season. Fort Lauderdale was the long-time home of the New York Yankees' spring training camp. Many of the players attended our church, and for several years I participated in a motivational Bible study with them every Tuesday night. In those days, the Yankee team stayed at the old Galt Ocean Mile Hotel in Fort Lauderdale. Their general manager was Clyde King. Clyde pitched for the old Brooklyn Dodgers in the late 40's and had been the manager of not only the New York Yankees, but the Atlanta Braves and the San Francisco Giants, as well. It was a great treat to sit outside in the evenings around the pool at that hotel and listen to all the baseball stories that were shared. But it was never a greater treat than when Yogi Berra, the homespun philosopher of baseball, and World Series catcher, would make his appearance. Yogi is famous for his inimitable way of coining a phrase. For example, he reminds us that, "It is never over 'til it's over." Once, when ordering a pizza, he was asked if he wanted it cut into twelve slices. Yogi replied, "No, cut it into eight. I can't eat 12!" When he was the field manager, he directed the outfielders by saying, "Go out into left field and pair off in threes." It was also Yogi who said, "It's *déjà vu* all over again." An interesting exchange occurred when the New York Yankees were playing the old Milwaukee Braves in the World Series. Yogi was known for his endless chatter behind the plate. He was constantly talking to his team and others. His purpose was two-fold: to motivate his own team, and distract the other team. Hank Aaron, the renowned all-time homerun leader, came to the plate. Yogi sought to distract him by yelling, "Hank, you're holding the bat wrong. The trademark needs to be face up so you can read it." Hank Aaron never said a word. He simply hit the next pitch over the left field fence for a homerun. As he trotted around the bases and crossed home plate, he looked at Yogi and said, "I didn't come here to read." Hank Aaron had started with his goal in mind and he stayed on track! Some of us have never homered in life because we have gotten off track. Perhaps we took our eye off the ball and lost our focus.

Nehemiah gives us some important steps that will enable us to stay on track. How can we do it? First, keep faith in God. As believers, our ultimate success is not in our own ability, in the workers around us, or in the king. Listen to Nehemiah, "The God of heaven Himself will prosper us" (Neh. 2:20). This is what keeps us going in our rebuilding process. This is what should keep our focus. God is with us, and the God of heaven Himself will prosper us. In times of my own personal discouragement, this is what has kept me going.

Second, Nehemiah reminds us to keep a servant's heart. He says, "…we His servants" (Neh. 2:20). Our Lord reminds us that if we want to be great in His kingdom we need to become the servant of all. When I came to be the pastor of the First Baptist Church in Dallas and began the rebuilding process there, I kept a verse of scripture on my phone and desk at all times. Every day I looked at that verse dozens of times. It was the promise of God from I Kings 12:7, "If you will be a servant to these people today, and serve them, and answer them, and speak good words to them, then they will be your servants forever." Keeping a servant's heart will keep us on track.

It is not only important to keep our faith in God and keep a servant's heart, but next, Nehemiah calls upon us to get busy with the task. He says, "…therefore we His servants will arise and build" (Neh. 2:20). We are to get busy doing what we know we should do. This will keep us on track. If we are in sales, then we know we should be making calls. Get busy with the task. Don't let anything keep you from it. If you have a marriage that needs to be rebuilt, it's easier to act your way into a new way of feeling than to feel your way into a new way of acting. How can we stay on track? Keep faith in God, keep a servant's heart, and get busy with the task.

Finally, Nehemiah reminds us to see our critics for what they are. Hear him as he says to his accusers, "…you have no heritage or right or memorial in Jerusalem" (Neh. 2:20). He boldly confronts his critics and refuses to play their game. He uses a "get tough" policy at just the right time. Leaders have to do this from time to time. It goes with the turf. If we don't do it we'll get off track. These men did not have the well-being of Jerusalem in mind. Nehemiah 2:10 attests to this when they were *disturbed* that "a man had come to seek the well-being of the children of Israel."

There will always be a Sanballat or a Tobiah to get you off track. There will always be someone or some thing that seeks to divert your focus. See them for what they are and don't let them get you off track. Some criticism is justified and should be evaluated and valued, but often it is only there to take away your focus and get you off track.

Nehemiah did not argue with the opposition, nor was he discouraged by it. He confronted them head-on and said, "You have no heritage or right or memorial in Jerusalem." So bug off. Nehemiah knew he and the people were about God's work. He wouldn't listen to anyone who was actively opposed to what he knew was right. And he didn't give his time to those who were in the way of where God was moving. He stayed on track.

I often wonder how many times those vocal critics who oppose something new stymie the work of God. They often say, "Why, we have lived with these walls for years. We're used to them now. We don't want to change them." Nehemiah planted his feet firmly and built a team spirit. A wise leader evaluates criticism in light of the spirit and attitude in which it is given, and stays on track!

Rebuilders build a team spirit before they see the fruition of their vision. They teach us to start with our goal in mind, to know where we are going, and how we are going to get there. They challenge us to seize our opportunities and walk through doors that are open for us. They call upon us to make a careful analysis of our situation, to see if there are any broken down walls in our own experience. They motivate us to get off dead center. How? By causing us to face up – team up – gird up – and look up.

Finally, they challenge us to "stay on track." Perhaps someone is reading these words that needs to get back on track today. The Lord Jesus Christ wants you on His team. He chose you! He wants to be your rebuilder. He wants to be the agent that rebuilds your life or whatever it is around you that may be broken. He has a goal for you, a vision of what He wants you to be with Him. You can conceive it, you can believe it, and you can achieve it...with His help. He is in the process of building team spirit and reminding us all that...*it's never too late for a new beginning.*

Part III

Rebuilders let go without letting up

NEHEMIAH has been teaching us some valuable lessons on rebuilding. We have looked and learned as he *started right,* and *built a team spirit.* We left him and his people in Part Two saying, "Let us rise up and build" (Neh. 2:18). This is not simply a lot of pumped-up mental attitude or a bunch of hype. These are not idle words. In Chapter Three of Nehemiah, we see the people "setting their hands to the work." The walls are going up. Rebuilding is on the way.

In reading the book of Nehemiah in the Old Testament, many people skip over Chapter Three. It is described as boring by some. On the surface, we see endless names that are hard to pronounce, and for the most part unknown. For example, consider these names found in one of the verses: Hananiah, Shelemiah, Hanun, Meshullam, Berechiah. These are not your basic household names, even in the Old Testament. Most of the names in the third chapter of Nehemiah are never before, and never again, mentioned in scripture. It has the appearance of all the excitement of a lifeless genealogy table. In fact, some writers and devotional commentators completely ignore Chapter Three when expounding on the message from Nehemiah. One famous Bible teacher and successful author of our day, in his otherwise fine book on Nehemiah, made no mention of Chapter Three. He deals with it as though the chapter does not even exist. One popular publishing company has a discussion guide that accompanies its commentary on Nehemiah. At the beginning of Nehemiah Chapter Three it says, "If your time is limited, this is a better chapter to skip than others." Many pay no attention whatsoever to this chapter, and either skip it completely, or skim it quickly, and turn the page to Chapter Four as the story of rebuilding the walls continues. However, I contend that the third chapter of Nehemiah is one of the most important chapters in the whole book. In this chapter, we discover one of the real secrets to Nehemiah's success. We discover his secret that will enable the work to be completed in just 52 days. What is it? It is the art of delegation!

Nehemiah *let go without letting up.* I want to repeat that. *He let go without letting up!* He came back to Jerusalem to be the rebuilder of the broken walls, but he knew he could not do the job alone. So, after *getting started right,* and *building a team spirit,* he now *delegates the task to others.* He lets go of ownership in the project, but does not let up on his passion or his commitment to see it through and to hold others accountable.

Delegation is the real secret to success, no matter what we are attempting to rebuild. In preparation for the writing of this volume, I read several motivational and business books on today's market; however, the Book of Nehemiah is by far the best of them all. Long before the modern success gurus wrote about the need to delegate, we read these time-tested principles here in Nehemiah Chapter Three. He teaches us the importance of *letting go without letting up.*

Nehemiah, no doubt, learned these principles of delegation from the Jewish Torah. Moses spoke of it and put it into practice. He was perplexed with the children of Israel in the wilderness, and spent his time judging and advising the people all by himself (Ex. 18). Jethro, his father-in-law, came upon the scene and watched men and women stand in line all day to seek counsel from Moses. He watched his son-in-law deal with each one of them, and saw at the end of the day that not only was Moses drained, but the people were drained themselves. Jethro gave him some great advice. He encouraged Moses to select from the people men who feared God, men of truth, to delegate this task. Moses began to *let go without letting up.* He "chose able men out of all Israel, and made them heads over the people: rulers of thousands, rulers of hundreds, rulers of fifties, and rulers of tens" (Ex. 18:25). And the result was, the job was done better and much more efficiently. Three thousand years have not lessened the importance of delegation. Our Lord Himself was a master delegator. On a Galilean mountainside, He did not personally feed the multiplied thousands. What did He do? He had the people sit down in rows, and distributed to the twelve, who distributed to the people. The rebuilder who does not discover this principle of delegation, who does not *let go without letting up,* will never be all that he or she can be.

An interesting thing happens when we take the time to read all of the names in Nehemiah Chapter Three. There are dozens mentioned, but Nehemiah's name is not one of them. He is the master delegator. He *lets go* but he doesn't *let up.*

Many never get started in rebuilding because they never discover this principle of delegation. Quite honestly, some confuse the issue. Some think to delegate means to dictate, so they bark orders and keep people under their thumbs. They always insist on their way. These are the types of leaders who can't let go, and can't let up. The result is lower morale for all involved. It happens in the home. It happens in the office. It can happen on a team; it can even happen in a church. In the home, dictators leave no room for team efforts. At the office, dictators give ultimatums and squelch innovation and creativity. They must control everything; they can't let go and they can't let up.

Others think to delegate means to abdicate. That is, they assign a task and not only let go, but they let up. There is no passion of follow-up. They never hold anyone accountable. Thus, things never get done nor finished. Abdicators are quick to place the blame on fellow workers to whom the task is assigned. While dictators don't let go nor let up, abdicators let go, and they also let up. They abdicate their place of leadership.

Look at Nehemiah as he steps on center stage. The effective leader does not relinquish his responsibility for exercising control. He may let go, but he never lets up. To delegate does not mean to abdicate our responsibility, nor does it mean to dictate to others. One of the things that distinguishes true rebuilders from those who only talk and never seem to get the job done, is the secret we find in Nehemiah Chapter Three – the ability to delegate, to *let go without letting up.*

For over a quarter of a century, I had the wonderful privilege of pastoring some great churches. Quite honestly, there were a number of jobs around that I could have done full time. Studying to preach was a full-time job; pastoring those in need of comfort and care was a full time job; counseling those who were troubled or confused was a full time job; contacting those in need of Christ and the church was a full-time job; administrating multi-million dollar budgets and ministerial staffs that numbered in the scores was a full-time job. I could dictate. I could abdicate. However, I chose to delegate. The only way the rebuilding process works in life is through delegation. This is true no matter what we may be rebuilding.

How did Nehemiah do it? How did he *let go without letting up?* Better yet, how can you and I *let go without letting up?* Nehemiah Chapter Three shows us the way. He lays out five important principles to accomplish the task of delegation. He says, "Set clear objectives with specific tasks, pick the right person for the right job, be an example yourself, hold people accountable, and give a genuine pat on the back." He faced an awesome task. Jerusalem had been deteriorating for scores of years. However, Nehemiah knew…*it's never too late for a new beginning!*

Chapter Ten

Set clear objectives with specific tasks

NEHEMIAH has been clear about his objectives throughout his book. His primary objective was to rebuild the walls of Jerusalem and repair its gates. There was no doubt about this. He had returned to Jerusalem, shared his vision, and the people adopted it, and said, "Let us rise up and build" (Neh. 2:18). Now, in Nehemiah Chapter Three, he assigns some specific tasks. Some of the workers were to hang certain gates. Others were to work on certain sections of the wall. It was to be a team effort, so Nehemiah set clear objectives with specific tasks. He was *letting go without letting up.* Each person knew exactly where he or she was to be along the wall. They each knew their own responsibility and what was expected of them. For example, "Then Eliashib the high priest rose up with his brethren the priests and built the Sheep Gate; they consecrated it and hung its doors. They built as far as the Tower of the Hundred, and consecrated it, then as far as the Tower of Hananel" (Neh. 3:1). On and on as the verses of Chapter Three unfold, we find Nehemiah setting clear objectives with specific tasks.

There was no one person who could rebuild the over two miles of broken down wall. But when Nehemiah divided the sections into about 40 segments, and delegated the work to dozens of leaders along the wall, the work was done in record time. Nehemiah set clear objectives with specific tasks. *He let go without letting up.* He was letting go of the ownership of the project, but not letting up on overseeing it to completion. One of the reasons so many of us have unfinished business in the work of rebuilding relationships, or homes, or self-confidence, is because we have no clear objectives with specific tasks.

There is a phrase we find recurring in nearly every verse of Nehemiah Chapter Three. Over and over again we read, "Next to him," "Next to them," "After him," "After them." All along the wall men and women had clear objectives with specific tasks. The words form a striking picture of unity in the midst of diversity. All along the wall men and women were working together with one accord. They were all going the same way, with clear objectives and specific tasks.

One of the all-time great television sitcoms was among the pioneers of that medium of media. Many of us remember *The Honeymooners,* starring Jackie Gleason. Gleason played Ralph Kramden, the bus driver. His friend and neighbor was Ed Norton, who worked in the sewer department of the local municipality. In one episode I remember seeing as a youngster, Ralph was trying to get a big piece of furniture through his apartment door. Ed walks by on his way home from work, lunch pail in hand. "Hey Ralph, can I give you a hand?" asked Ed. Upon the affirmative reply, Ed Norton, clad in white tee shirt and vest and rumpled hat, takes hold of the furniture outside the door while Ralph has the furniture inside the door. They strain and pull and push, but the furniture doesn't budge. It's still right there in the middle of the doorway. This goes on for several minutes. Finally Ralph stops, wipes his brow, and exclaims, "I don't think we're ever going to get this furniture in the apartment." "Get it *in* the apartment?" questions Norton. "I thought we were trying to get it *out* of the apartment!"

How important it is for Nehemiah and his workers to be moving together, to *have clear objectives with specific tasks.* And how important for any of us who are in the process of rebuilding. We are all "next to" someone in the rebuilding process, and we all need each other as we work together in the business of rebuilding.

Setting clear objectives with specific tasks is the first principle of delegation. It's a very difficult thing to delegate a task to someone else if they do not have a clear objective regarding it. Along Jerusalem's walls were specific jobs to be done by specific people. Someone was responsible for each section of the wall. Those who worked in groups had someone over them (Neh. 3:13). The power to make decisions was delegated to each group. Nehemiah *let go, but he didn't let up.*

We never rebuild relationships without clear objectives with specific tasks. This is certainly true in the husband-wife relationship. Each of us has a specific task. It's also true in rebuilding our lives, our businesses, or our churches. Somewhere there is a place on the wall that no one can fill like you can.

Look at Nehemiah. He is letting go. He is not trying to do it all, but he is not letting up. How does he delegate? First, he sets clear objectives with specific tasks.

What is your objective in rebuilding? Are you trying to rebuild a marriage, or a church, or a business, or a life? Do you have a specific task upon which to work? This might be at the very core of your problem. How do we let go without letting up? We begin by setting clear objectives with specific tasks. *It's never too late for a new beginning.*

Chapter Eleven

Pick the right person
for the right job

PICKING the right person for the right job is essential in the task of delegation, of *letting go without letting up.* Nehemiah was a master at seeing the need for this. He placed people near their own homes (Neh. 3:23, 28). This was a family effort. Think about it. If you were working close to your own home you might take more of a personal interest. You might take the task of rebuilding those walls a little bit more seriously than you would if you were somewhere else. You might be a little more highly motivated to see the job to completion. This way no one had to commute to the other side of Jerusalem. Nehemiah was saving valuable time and energy. Where there appeared to be no residents living nearby the wall, Nehemiah stationed people from the outlying towns like Tekoa and Jericho to those particular places. He was wise. He knew the best place to start to rebuild was at your own home.

Nehemiah *let go without letting up.* How? He *set clear objectives with specific tasks,* and he *picked the right person for the right job.* Some removed the rubbish. Others cut the stone. Some stacked the debris. Others laid the stones in place along the wall. Somewhere there was a job for everyone. There was a specific place to use the gifts and abilities of everyone. All the way up and down the wall this principle played out. There was even a place for "the priest." One might think they would bow out of work and be about the duties in the temple, but to their credit, they led the way in rebuilding. And note the job that Nehemiah gave them. They were to repair the Sheep Gate (Neh. 3:1). This was important to them, for it was the gate through which people brought their sacrifices to the temple. Nehemiah picked the right person for the right job. Some never learn to delegate because they have the wrong person in the right job, or the right person in the wrong job.

There were also "goldsmiths" who worked with intricate details, and yet they had a place to lay large stones in the wall. Nehemiah 3:23 said there were "bachelors" working on the wall. Even though they had no family to protect, they were in their place. There were single adults on the wall who had the task of rebuilding a section of the wall that no one could build like they could. It is also important to note there were men from Tekoa and Jericho, as much as twenty miles away, who had nothing to gain personally, but were there in their place. There were also "politicians" along the wall (Neh. 3:9, 12), the big wigs, the VIPs of Jerusalem. Everyone got their hands dirty. There were women who were doing their share. There were those who had failed marriages. In Nehemiah 3:11, we are introduced to a man that Ezra tells us had been previously married to a pagan wife. Now he and his family surface again. He didn't drop out. He found forgiveness, and there was an important spot there on the wall for him. The mistakes of the past didn't keep those men and women in Jerusalem from rebuilding the walls, and they shouldn't keep us from rebuilding our broken down walls.

In Nehemiah Chapter Two, he had talked about how "the hand of God" had been upon him. Now God is at work through the "hands of the people." They "set their hands to this good work" (Neh. 2:18). There was a job for each of them to do. Nehemiah set clear objectives with specific tasks, and picked the right people for the right jobs.

Somewhere in the process of rebuilding, there is a job for you that no one else can do quite like you. Somewhere along the wall is a section that God has assigned to you. Nehemiah *let go without letting up.* How? He began by setting clear objectives with specific tasks so that everyone would know exactly what was expected of them. Then he picked the right person for the right job because he knew…*it's never too late for a new beginning!*

Chapter Twelve

Be an example yourself

WE WILL never get others to follow us in the home, in the office, or anywhere else, unless we lead by example. This is exactly what Nehemiah did. He was "hands on" in his leadership style. Even though he omitted his own name in this exhaustive list, he was as active as anyone was, and even more so. He was a true leader. He led by example. Nehemiah inspired those people to work by getting his own hands dirty. He was right there with them. He was working. He was sweating. How do we know? Because when we come to Chapter Four we will read Nehemiah 4:21,23, which says, "So we labored in the work, and half of the men held the spears from daybreak until the stars appeared …neither I, my brethren, my servants, nor the men of the guard who followed me took off our clothes, except that everyone took them off for washing."

If we want people to follow, we must lead by example. This is one of the great principles of leadership. We see it all through the Bible, and outside the Bible, when anyone rises to the level of effective leadership. The most poignant leadership statement to be found is the one made by Gideon when, about to face the

Midianite hosts, he turned to his men and said, "Do as I do!" (Judg. 7:17). As a young man, my pastor, Dr. W. Fred Swank, always ingrained in me that I should never ask my people to do anything that I was not there doing with them.

Nehemiah was wise enough to know that he would never be able to delegate effectively if he was not in the trenches himself. *He let go, but he didn't let up.* He set clear objectives with specific tasks; he picked the right person for the right job; and he led by example. *It's never too late for a new beginning.*

Chapter Thirteen

Hold people accountable

TALK about accountability…Nehemiah knew who worked next to whom. He knew who did what work. He knew who did not do what work. He even reports for all posterity that "the Tekoites made repairs; but their nobles did not put their shoulders to the work of their Lord" (Neh. 3:5). He also took note of who did extra work. "The Tekoites repaired another section" (Neh. 3:27). He held his people accountable. Accountability is essential if we ever expect to learn the art of delegation. There will always be those who will not want to get their hands dirty. There will always be those who will not support the work of rebuilding and will refuse to participate in it. This was true with Nehemiah. After recording the neglect of some of them in Nehemiah 3:5, he just went right on with his task. He moved with the movers! He stayed on track and remained optimistic in the task of rebuilding. He did not let those who faltered along the way discourage him. He worked with those who caught the vision, and held them accountable for their assigned tasks. This enabled him to succeed in what many thought was an impossible task.

Many never rebuild because accountability is a lost word in the process. Perhaps this is the single reason why so many marriages are never rebuilt. It is the reason so many relationships are broken. The lack of accountability also explains why some businesses falter while others flourish.

I drive an Oldsmobile that wonderfully accomplishes the primary purpose of getting me to my destination. I took it back to the shop recently for a regular checkup. There was nothing wrong with it, but it was time for a checkup. My wife and I are fortunate to own our own home. Some time ago, we had some repairs done to the roof. It wasn't leaking, but some of the eaves were beginning to rot. I live in a body that is deteriorating with age. Fortunately, there is nothing wrong with it, but I go every year for a complete physical. What generally goes wrong with my car, my house, or my body, does so because of one word – neglect. No accountability. If accountability is good for cars, and homes, and physical needs, it is essential for the process of rebuilding. In fact, rebuilders *let go, but they don't let up.* They hold people accountable.

Nehemiah is the master rebuilder. He got started right, and built a team spirit. Now he accelerates the process by letting go without letting up. He sets clear objectives with specific tasks, picks the right people for the right jobs, leads by example, and holds people accountable. He knows…*it's never too late for a new beginning.*

Chapter Fourteen

Give a genuine pat on the back

NEHEMIAH took note of what was going on and went up and down the wall patting men and women on the back. There is a recurring expression throughout Chapter Three. He continues to say that certain individuals "repaired another section" (Neh. 3:11, 19, 21, 24, 27, 30). He not only knew who they were and where they were, but what they did. He recorded it for all posterity, especially those who went the second mile and repaired another section besides the one assigned to them. In so doing, he rebuilt the walls and developed a tremendous amount of loyalty and team spirit with his people. He saw the importance of giving a genuine pat on the back.

Nehemiah did not play favorites. Some had bigger tasks than others. However, he complimented each of them on the accomplishment of their assigned task. For example, in verse 13, we find a group of men and women working together and rebuilding 1500 feet of broken walls. This is equivalent to the length of five football fields. Right next to them, (Neh. 3:14) there was a guy hard at work on the Refuse Gate who single-handedly repaired it alone. Nehemiah also makes note of the fact that some of the people did what was required, and "then some"(Neh. 3:11, 19, 21, 24, 27, 30). He gives them a pat on the back for the extra effort that was above and beyond the call of duty, and he records it for all posterity.

Nehemiah especially singles out a man by the name of Baruch in verse twenty. He noted that he "carefully" repaired his section. I can see Nehemiah stopping by his side as he moves along the wall, kneeling down. "Great job!" He makes a note to record for all posterity, and here we are, 2000 years later, talking about Baruch today. I am sure when Nehemiah encouraged him, patted him on the back, and noted that he "carefully" worked on his particular task, Baruch went above and beyond the call of duty. Nehemiah was *building team spirit,* and *letting go without letting up.*

Perhaps there is no greater motivation for those to whom the work is delegated than genuine appreciation and encouragement. We live in a day of increasing depersonalization. Many of us are nothing but a number to a mammoth, centralized government. We are simply a social security number. To the census bureau, we are nothing but a statistic. Nehemiah is showing us the need to take a personal interest in those on our team at home, in the office, in the church, or wherever we may be. He knew their names. He treated them as valuable coworkers. He let them know he believed they have worth. In his mind, each of them was as important as the next one in line. They were not a *group* to Nehemiah. They were individuals. And he knew the importance of giving a genuine pat on the back.

Each of us needs to feel we are worth something. This was certainly true in Jerusalem. They had been dejected and defeated for years, and had passed by the rubble of the broken walls every day knowing something should be done. Has anyone reading these pages been walking that way today? Do you keep telling yourself that someday you are going to do something about the broken walls around you?

Affirmation is the single most effective way to rebuild. It is the greatest motivating factor I know. In the home, every child needs to know that dad believes in him. Every student needs to know the teacher believes in him. Every worker needs to know the boss believes in him. Every wife needs to know the husband believes in her.

After reading Chapter Three, it dawns on us that Nehemiah never mentions himself by name here. He doesn't mention where he works or what he did. He's not looking for praise from others. He is too busy going up and down the wall, helping here and there, giving encouragement, a pat on the back here, a pat on the back there. "We can do it!" "Keep it up!" "You're doing great!" He knew how important it was to let go without letting up. Nehemiah is the master delegator. He didn't dictate to his people and go up and down the wall with a whip in his hand, berating or criticizing their tasks. Nor did he abdicate and simply leave them to their own. Look at him. *He's letting go without letting up!*

Those in the process of rebuilding will do one of three things. They will either delegate, dictate, or abdicate. Those who are successful let go without letting up. How? They learn from Nehemiah. *They set clear objectives with specific tasks. They pick the right persons for the right job. They are an example themselves. They hold people accountable, and they give a genuine pat on the back.*

We have learned how to get started right by making an

honest evaluation, identifying with the need, taking personal responsibility, and leaving our comfort zones. We have learned how to build a team spirit by starting with our goal in mind, seizing our opportunities, making a careful analysis of our situation, motivating our people to get off dead center, and staying on track. Now it's time for those in the process of rebuilding to find a place on the wall and do the job that no one else can do. Not everyone was supposed to work on the Sheep Gate, but some of them were. Not everyone was to hang the gates, but some of them were. There is a place on the wall for each of us.

In the process of rebuilding, delegation is the key. This is exactly the way the Lord Jesus Christ builds His church. How? He delegates. He assigns tasks and delegates duties. He appoints pastors and undershepherds. He appoints deacons to stand by the pastor. He assigns some to be teachers, and gifts others to perform the works of ministry. He is interested in rebuilding our lives today. We are not puppets. He does not dictate to us, nor does He abdicate. He lets go, but He doesn't let up. He wants us to know...*it's never too late for a new beginning.*

Part IV

Rebuilders understand "YAC" is what really matters

"YAC" is a new word in the vocabulary of all football fans across America. It is a new statistic that recently was introduced into the National Football League to help determine the success of a power runner. YAC is an acrostic that stands for "yards after contact." The great running backs in recent pro football history have been measured by the yards they've gained after an opposing player initially contacted them. In Emmitt Smith's great years as a running back for the Dallas Cowboys, he set all kinds of records, including most touchdowns in a season. He has truly been one of the greatest running backs of all time. But few people know that he also led the league in this little-known statistic, YAC. YAC was coined by John Madden, the former professional coach, and now television network analyst. He has compiled this new measurement by counting the number of yards a runner makes after an opposing player hits him.

The next time you have opportunity to watch a professional football game on television, look for this particular statistic. When an opposing player hits a running back, he doesn't stop, throw the ball down, and quit. He doesn't cave in, crumble on the ground, and then stroll back to the huddle. He doesn't let go of the ball and fumble away his opportunity. He doesn't turn around and run in the opposite direction. What does he do? He keeps his legs churning after he is hit; he keeps moving forward; he keeps heading toward the goal line. The great runners make most of their yards after the initial contact. They score most of their touchdowns after they have already been hit. They simply keep moving forward.

Some of us never rebuild in life because as soon as we meet opposition, we quit. We go back to the huddle. Some of us just simply lay down, while others let go of the ball and fumble. Some even run in the opposite direction from the opposition. But rebuilders keep moving forward after they are hit. It is the YAC (yards after contact) that matters most in life, not just in football. Often the YAC is what determines whether we score a touchdown. It is the single element that separates some from others. YAC is the ability to keep going when we are confronted with obstacles and opposition in conflict.

Perhaps someone is reading this volume today who has stopped rebuilding because of meeting opposition. Perhaps you were building a broken relationship and conflict came. It was so easy to simply exclaim, "What's the use?" It was just easier to quit. Remember, it's the YAC that makes the difference in life. Some are rebuilding their self-confidence and go along fairly well, and then out of nowhere get hit and are tempted to quit. The same is true whether we are rebuilding a marriage, a business, or whatever. YAC is what enables us to overcome our obstacles.

Nehemiah led his league in "yards after contact." In fact, this is one of the real secrets to his own success. As we turn our pages to Nehemiah Chapter Four, we see him confronted with opposition from without, but also opposition from within. However, Nehemiah is a true rebuilder, and he leaves us with some valuable lessons in learning how to overcome our obstacles. You may get started right, as Nehemiah did, and you may build a team spirit, as he also did. You may even learn how to let go without letting up by emulating his delegation skills. However, when it comes to rebuilding, you will never reach the goal if you do not learn how to deal with opposition, how to overcome your obstacles, and how to gain yardage after you have been hit. Anyone who gets serious about rebuilding will meet opposition. Like ham and eggs, steak and potatoes, corned beef and cabbage, rebuilding and opposition go hand in hand. Sometimes it comes from without. A Sanballat or a Tobiah will rise up against you, as they did against Nehemiah. Other times it comes from within. Judah, of all people, was about to give up on Nehemiah. Sometimes, like Nehemiah, you find that someone on your own team is the opponent. How we deal with opposition that comes our way will determine the success or failure of our own rebuilding projects. Remember, it's the YAC, "yards after contact", that matter most.

In Chapter Four, when confronted with opposition, Nehemiah did four things that enabled him to be an overcomer and finish the job God had called him to perform. He keeps making yards after contact. How? To begin with, he shows us how important it is to deal with conflict head-on. Don't think it is going away if we simply ignore it. We must meet our conflict head-on and deal with it. We cannot turn around and run the other way and still get the business of rebuilding accomplished.

Second, Nehemiah overcame his obstacles by making proper adjustments. There was still a lot of rubbish that needed to be removed around the walls of Jerusalem. To attempt to rebuild the walls on a foundation as shabby as rubbish would only mean the wall would one day crumble again. From time to time in the rebuilding process, we have to call a timeout and make some proper adjustments to our own game plan.

Next, Nehemiah overcame his obstacles by keeping on doing what was right. Once he had dealt with conflict head-on and made some proper adjustments, he simply kept doing what was right. He watched and worked. With a trowel in one hand and a sword in the other, he continued with the process of rebuilding, while keeping a keen eye out for opposition. He did not let the opposition deter him from the task that was ahead. He kept doing what was right.

Finally, Nehemiah overcame those obstacles by rallying his troops. It is important in rebuilding to keep everyone's eye on the goal. He not only began with his goal in mind, but he continued in the same vein. Remember, it is the YAC that makes the difference in rebuilding. *It's never too late for a new beginning.*

Chapter Fifteen

Deal with conflict head-on

NEHEMIAH got started right, built a team spirit, let go without letting up, and now he faces the biggest challenge of all — opposition. Don't think when you get serious about rebuilding that you'll be able to do so without opposition. In Nehemiah's case, it was persistent (Neh. 2:10, 19; 4:1-2, 7-8; 6:1-2). Do not fool yourself into thinking that opposition will go away. Our challenge is in learning to deal with it, and overcome it. Nehemiah, like Emmitt Smith and other great running backs today, dealt with conflict head-on. He knew it was the YAC that would matter most in the rebuilding process.

As is often the case with opposition, it came from without (Neh. 4:1-3), and from within (Neh. 4:10). Note that outside opposition first came in the form of mocking and ridicule. When Sanballat heard that Nehemiah was rebuilding the walls, he became furious and indignant and "mocked the Jews." He asked, "What are these feeble Jews doing? Will they fortify themselves? Will they offer sacrifices? Will they complete it in a day?" (Neh. 4:1-2). Then Tobiah got his two cents in, "Whatever they build, if even a fox goes up on it, he will break down their stone wall" (Neh. 4:3). This outside opposition of mocking and ridicule attacked Nehemiah at the point of his morale, his motives, and his mission. They called him and his coworkers "feeble Jews" (Neh. 4:2). Sanballat was attacking the morale of the Jews. He was attempting to demolish their self-worth. He was attempting to weaken their resolve. Have you ever met anyone like Sanballat? Here we are in the midst of a rebuilding process. Our walls are going up, and someone comes along and says something that hits at our morale. Perhaps someone put you down, and you are tempted to say, "What's the use?" Remember, it's YAC, the "yards after contact", that determines the real winners in rebuilding.

Next, Nehemiah's motives are attacked. They said that he and his Jewish friends were simply doing it "for themselves" (Neh. 4:2). The enemy implies that Nehemiah has a selfish motive in what he is doing. The Sanballats of this world cannot understand why you or I would do something for God's glory alone. If you are in the process of rebuilding, don't be surprised if someone sees your walls going up and begins to attack not only your morale, but also begins to question your motives. When this happens, simply remember it's the YAC that really matter most.

They also attacked Nehemiah's mission. They began to question whether he would ever really finish the job and revive those stones from the rubble. They even said, "If a fox jumped upon the wall, it was so poorly constructed it would fall down" (Neh. 4:3). Tobiah chimed in by implying that the job was simply just too big for them. Often the task seems impossible. When this happens, there is a Tobiah in our experience that usually jumps in and begins to attack our mission.

What is the real issue here? Sanballat and Tobiah simply

did not like to see those walls going up. Habitual critics always resist change. When we read the text in Nehemiah Chapter Four, it is interesting to see how these types of people flock together. Nehemiah was dealing with conflict head-on.

I often wonder about the work of God that never causes the enemy to raise his head in opposition. The truth is, any time someone takes God at His word and begins to rebuild something of value, there will be a Sanballat or a Tobiah to mock, and ridicule, and attack our morale, our motive, and our mission.

For example, we believe the way to rebuild a broken home is for the husband to assume the role of the spiritual leader. God designed the home to have a head. Tell that to our modern world, and listen to them mock and ridicule those of us who take the husband's spiritual headship from the Bible as truth. Sanballats and Tobiahs are all around us today. Anyone who stands upon the word of God will find opposition from without, and, in a sense, should consider it a badge of honor.

When you are in the process of rebuilding, there will always be someone asking the question, "Will you complete the wall?" We should not be surprised when we have opposition from without. What should be done about it? We should learn from Nehemiah, and deal with conflict head-on.

Opposition not only comes from without, but it also comes from within (Neh. 4:10). The opposition from without did not have much effect. It did demoralize some, but not many. Now the tribe of Judah is ready to lie down on the job after being hit by opposition. Judah said the strength of the laborers was failing, and there was so much rubbish it was doubtful they would ever be able to accomplish the task. Those words have a haunting sound. Of all the people – Judah! Judah was the strongest of the tribes of whom the Bible says, "The scepter shall not depart from Judah, nor a lawgiver from between his feet, until Shiloh comes" (Gen. 49:10).

What happened? Fatigue, frustration, and failure plagued them. Fatigue was a contributing factor to their frustration. They said, "The strength of the laborers is failing" (Neh. 4:10). They had been working so hard at the task that they tired of it. They were physically depleted. We are not talking about small "Acme bricks" here. Anyone who has ever been to the Holy Land is always astounded at how those massive stones that make up the walls of Jerusalem could have been put in place in such an ancient culture. No wonder their strength was failing. Fatigue had set in, and with it had come discouragement. This is often at the root of a lot of our own failures. We simply give out and become too tired to go on, so we give in and are tempted to give up. When fatigue sets in, we begin to lose our perspective, and little things become bigger than they are.

Frustration was another factor. Judah said, "There is so much rubbish." The magnitude of the task was astounding. They looked at the debris, so massive all around. There was so much to be cleared away. They lost their enthusiasm. They lost their vision. They took their eye off the goal and put it on all the rubbish. Those who are in the process of rebuilding are often tempted to do this. There are times when we are tempted to look at the sheer massiveness of our task. When we focus upon the rubbish alone, it will bring frustration, as it did with Judah.

Fatigue and frustration are most generally followed by failure. Judah went on, "We are not able to build the wall." They lost confidence. Is anyone reading this volume feeling that way today? You started out on the process of rebuilding. You got started right, built a team spirit, and then fatigue and frustration led to failure.

It is important to remember that the Jews were at the halfway point at this particular time. "So we built the wall, and the entire wall was joined together up to half its height" (Neh. 4:6). Incidentally, that is a dangerous place to be in the process of rebuilding. Often it is the most discouraging place along the journey. There may be some man reading this volume who is at the midpoint of life. Your wall is built half way, but you are not where you thought you should be. Thus, you are discouraged, and perhaps in frustration are saying, "We are not able to build the wall." And so you are tempted to run the other way. Remember that YAC is what counts in life.

Listen to Judah. Perhaps, as you look at your own task of rebuilding it appears to be too big. Sometimes opposition from within comes in the form of "but." Yes, we built half the wall, "but" there is too much rubbish. Have you ever had someone agree with you on something, and then add "but?" "That's a great idea, BUT it can't be done." "That's a super suggestion, BUT it's never been done before." "That's a wonderful thought, BUT we don't have enough resources." When someone says that to you, don't believe the first part. You may as well discount everything before the "but." Their true response always follows the "but."

When rebuilding, the thing that hurts most is not opposition from without, but it's the opposition that comes from within. Even our Lord Jesus faced opposition from within His own close-knit group of followers. It is discouraging when someone from within says, "We can't!" It is one thing for those outside to stand in opposition, but quite another when those within our own ranks, like Judah, do so. Put yourself in Nehemiah's place. How would you respond? What kind of "yards after contact" average would you have in this particular game?

Here is opposition from without and from within. What did Nehemiah do? He dealt with conflict head-on. He persisted at his task. I like the way he says it in verse six, "So we built the wall." He just kept mixing the mortar. He kept laying the stones. He kept rebuilding the wall. Yes, it would have been easy for him to go back to Persia and get his old cushy job back, but he didn't. What did he do? He took his dilemma straight to the Lord (Neh. 4:4). Rebuilding the walls of Jerusalem was God's project, not Nehemiah's.

After he was initially hit with opposition, Nehemiah kept going. As he kept moving toward his goal, the opposition increased. Sanballat and Tobiah and their friends "became very angry, and all of them conspired together to come and attack Jerusalem and create confusion" (Neh. 4:7-8). Their enemy had surrounded them and was threatening violence. They got very angry at Nehemiah's success, and now sought to intimidate the Jews. Thus, these warring factions formed a conspiracy. It is amazing how suddenly people can bury their differences and come together against one particular person. The Lord Jesus suffered the same thing. He bore the brunt of ridicule and conspiracy, and the Bible records, "That very day Pilate and Herod became friends with each other, for previously they had been at enmity with each other" (Luke 23:12).

How did Nehemiah deal with his conflict head-on? He began in the place of prayer. He says, "We made our prayer to our God, and because of them we set a watch against them day and night" (Neh. 4:9). He prayed, and continued to work harder. Prayer was always a priority, but it was no substitute for action. What should you do when you meet opposition in rebuilding? You should certainly pray, and go ahead and deal with opposition head-on. Are you rebuilding a vocation? Then pray and fill out the resume. Beat the pavement. Make your contacts. Are you seeking to rebuild a marriage? First pray, and then do something. Begin to do the things you did at first.

Nehemiah dealt with conflict head-on. He just kept rebuilding the wall with "yards after contact." When he got hit with opposition he didn't quit. He didn't fold up on the ground. He didn't fumble. He didn't let go of the ball. He didn't run in the opposite direction. No! He kept moving forward toward his goal. This is the mark of a true overcomer and a true rebuilder. They deal with conflict head-on. They have an optimism that is contagious, and they persevere in the face of opposition.

It's one thing to get started right. In fact, it is essential. It's another thing to build a team spirit, to motivate and mobilize those around you. It's one thing to let go without letting up, to delegate the tasks. But the real issue in rebuilding comes in our ability to overcome our obstacles, to keep at it after we have been hit. To persevere in the face of opposition that strikes at our morale, our motive, and our mission. Yes, it is the YAC that makes the difference in life. Even though we may have been hit with opposition...*it's never too late for a new beginning!*

Chapter Sixteen

Make proper adjustments

OVER the course of my ministry, it has been my joy to pastor in major metropolitan areas that had professional athletic teams. Consequently, I have had numerous opportunities to lead Bible studies for various professional athletes, and speak to team chapel services before games. Some of my most memorable experiences have been with my friend, Mike Ditka, who at this writing is the coach of the New Orleans Saints. One of the secrets of Mike's success is to make proper adjustments during the course of the football game, particularly during the half time. This unique ability is essential not only in football games, but also in life circumstances and situations.

Nehemiah put his finger on the problem of his opposition when he indicated that some of the Jews were "dwelling too near the enemy" (Neh. 4:12). Judah had been listening to some of the Jews who were living "near the enemy." The enemy had influenced them. They picked up the gossip. They were far removed from the center glow of the spirit dynamic in the rebuilding of Jerusalem. Living near the enemy caused them to put their focus on the enemy itself.

They began to listen to them instead of God. I have seen this happen with people who are seeking to rebuild their lives. Some just simply stay out there dangerously close to the enemy, and will not move in near to the heart of where God is moving and rebuilding.

Note that those in Judah said there was simply "too much rubbish." It is a dangerous thing to try and build on rubbish. Many people are doing this today, especially those attempting to rebuild relationships. They never really remove the rubbish that has accumulated over the years; they simply try to build on top of it, only to see the wall crumble again, and again. To risk rebuilding on rubbish simply means that sooner or later the wall will fall again.

There was nothing wrong with the foundation upon which Nehemiah was building. It was still solid. The problem was that for all of those years junk and debris had accumulated on top of the foundation. It had piled up, and nothing had been done about it. To attempt to rebuild the walls of Jerusalem on such rubbish would have been futile. They may have gotten the walls up, but the first big wind or assault of any kind would have crumbled them again. Many of us in the process of rebuilding do not have to lay a new foundation. We simply need to remove the rubbish, expose the old foundation, and begin to build upon it again. Some have marriages that are built on a solid foundation, but rubbish has been piling up for years. We need to remove it, and get back to the foundation. This is why so many are up and down in relationships. They build up the walls only to see them fall again. We need to make proper adjustments, and remove the rubbish.

Some reading this volume have lives that were built on the solid foundation. You were brought up on the principles of the

Bible. You have a good foundation, but have not seen it for a while. You allowed rubbish to accumulate and pile up, and you simply need to remove it. Others continually try to keep rebuilding on rubbish; everything goes along well for a while, and then it falls again. Some are involved in an endless cycle, and the simple reason is they are building upon rubbish.

Nehemiah dealt with conflict head-on, and now he makes some proper adjustments. Listen to him as he regroups, "Do not be afraid of them. Remember the Lord, great and awesome, and fight for your brethren, your sons, your daughters, your wives, and your houses" (Neh. 4:14). Remember that it is halftime (Neh. 4:6). And now, Nehemiah makes some proper adjustments. He does the same thing a great coach would do. He gathers his troops at halftime, removes the rubbish, and makes proper adjustments. Nehemiah calls his people off the wall, rallies them together, huddles them up, and gives them an inspiring halftime talk.

Like a seasoned coach of a championship team, Nehemiah makes proper adjustments. There is a rebuke. "Do not be afraid of them." He addresses their fear. Then he encourages them. "Remember the Lord, great and awesome." He reminds them that the battle is really the Lord's. Then he exhorts them. "Fight for your brethren." Look at Nehemiah as he deals with conflict head-on, and now as he makes proper adjustments. Some of us are still trying to build upon rubbish. Remember, it's the YAC that makes the difference in life. As we continue to churn toward our goal, we will become more and more convinced… *it's never too late for a new beginning.*

Chapter Seventeen

Keep doing what is right

HAVING dealt with conflict head-on, and made the proper adjustments, now Nehemiah continues to do what is right. He simply puts it this way, "All of us returned to the wall, everyone to his work" (Neh. 4:15). They kept doing what was right (Neh. 4:15-17, 21-23). There is an important principle at work here. Nehemiah never left the rebuilding for the battle! We are often tempted to leave the rebuilding process and go to battle when opposition arises. It would have been easy for Nehemiah to have answered scorn with scorn, to leave the rebuilding for the battle, but he wisely resisted and simply kept doing what was right.

Look at Nehemiah. Here are "yards after contact." They mocked, but he kept rebuilding. They ridiculed, but he kept rebuilding. They threatened, but he kept rebuilding. They despised him, but he kept rebuilding. They conspired against him, but he kept rebuilding. He kept doing what was right.

To keep on doing what is right is a mighty principle. Half of Nehemiah's people watched while the other half worked. They kept doing what was right. This is the secret in rebuilding when we are confronted with opposition. The apostle Paul was a master at this. He had really good statistics when it came to "yards after contact." Listen to him, "We are hard-pressed on every side, yet not crushed; we are perplexed, but not in despair; persecuted, but not forsaken; struck down, but not destroyed" (II Cor.4:8-9) (Phillips Translation). I like that. Paul is saying "I get right back up and keep doing what is right!" It's the YAC that enables us to rebuild the broken walls around us.

Nehemiah concludes the chapter by saying, "So we labored in the work, and half of the men held the spears from daybreak until the stars appeared...So neither I, my brethren, my servants, nor the men of the guard who followed me took off our clothes, except that everyone took them off for washing" (Neh. 4:21, 23). Nehemiah keeps leading by example. He's done this all through his book, and he continues now. He is standing with his people through it all. He leads them by example to simply keep doing what is right. He has never been more aware that it is the YAC that makes the difference in life. *It's never too late for a new beginning.*

Chapter Eighteen

Rally the troops

WE ALL need a Nehemiah to encourage us to keep rebuilding. We all need a Nehemiah to rally the troops around us. Had it not been for Nehemiah, the Jews might have abandoned their task again and left the wall in shambles, as they had done for so many years. He dealt with conflict head-on; he made some proper adjustments; he kept doing what was right; and now he rallies the troops around him. One person can make a tremendous difference, as Nehemiah did.

Nehemiah had a rallying point for his whole team. He kept the trumpeter always at his side (Neh. 4:18). He said, "Whenever you hear the sound of the trumpet, rally to us there. Our God will fight for us" (Neh. 4:20). Do you get the picture? The workers were widely scattered all along the wall. They were laboring at the task of rebuilding. At the sound of the trumpet, they were to leave their work and rally around Nehemiah for the final overthrow of the enemy. The focal point of the whole strategy was their commander in chief and the trumpeter by his side, who would sound the signal to gather.

Do I need to say any more? Across the world today there

are preachers, and laborers, and missionaries, and others scattered all along the wall, rebuilding the kingdom of God. In some places, the ranks are thin. Some are way out there and so close to the enemy. Others are cut off from fellowship, but they are rebuilding. We all have one Commander in Chief, the Lord Jesus Christ, and He is the rallying point for all of us who are interested in rebuilding our lives. One day, He said, the trumpet will sound and we shall leave our work, put down our tools, and rally around Him. But, until then, we must keep rebuilding the wall. We must keep overcoming our obstacles. How? Deal with conflict head-on. Make proper adjustments. Keep doing what's right. And rally our troops.

I attended a basketball game recently where the home team had a huge lead. In the last quarter, the lead began to dwindle as the opposition became stronger and stronger, and the momentum changed. The home team was on the verge of losing its large lead, and with only a few minutes left the coach called a time out. He gathered his team around him. What did he do? He dealt with the conflict head-on. He made proper adjustments. He encouraged his team to keep doing what was right, and he rallied them to the task. They went out and won the ballgame. It may be that some of us simply need to call a "timeout" in life, and remember that it is the YAC that matters most.

Nehemiah reminded his people, "Our God will fight for us." He was rallying the troops. Sanballat and Tobiah had said, "You won't." Judah had said, "We can't." Nehemiah said, "God will." People begin to rally around something when they see God in it. Which voice is yours? Is it the voice of Sanballat? "You won't!" Is it the voice of Judah? "We can't!" Or, is it the voice of Nehemiah? "God will." There are three voices shouting at us from Nehemiah Chapter Four. The question is, to whose voice will we listen? Nehemiah said, "God will." And He did! "So the wall was finished in fifty-two days" (Neh. 6:15). Yes, Emmitt Smith was one of the great professional runners of all National Football League history, largely because of the statistic called YAC, "yards after contact." How do you rate in this category? It may well determine whether you rebuild or not.

In the early days of my pastorate at First Baptist Church in Dallas, I was often overwhelmed with the task. It was a tremendous challenge of rebuilding one of the great churches of America. At the time, my daughter was playing on the high school basketball team at our First Baptist Academy. I would constantly encourage her to take more shots. If I told her once, I told her a thousand times, "You can't make the basket if you don't shoot it." There was a particular time when I was feeling like Judah and wondering if there was so much rubbish that the task was insurmountable. A postcard came in the mail. It was from Holly, who by this time was in her first year of college. She wrote me some encouraging words, assuring me of her prayers. The card simply said, "OPPORTUNITY: YOU WILL MISS 100% OF THE SHOTS YOU DON'T TAKE!" It stayed on my desk the remaining years of that wonderful pastorate in Dallas.

Nehemiah is shouting to us, "Keep going! It's the YAC that matters most. Don't quit. Don't fumble. Take the shot. Don't lie down. Don't run the other way. Keep moving forward. You will miss 100% of the shots you don't take."

Is anyone reading these words that's about to give up? Take a "timeout." Remember that Christ is your coach. He is reminding you to deal with conflict head-on, to make some proper adjustments, to keep doing what's right. He's rallying his troops, and this includes you and me. Long before John Madden ever coined the phrase, Jesus showed us the importance of YAC. It is the "yards after contact" that matter most, and serve to remind us that...*it's never too late for a new beginning.*

Part V

Rebuilders never cut
what they can untie

Most of us had a vacant lot in our childhood that became the gathering place for all the neighborhood kids. We had some great ballgames in the old vacant lot where I grew up. That old sandy lot was like Yankee Stadium in my mind. Recently, I drove through the old neighborhood. The houses and yards that once were so well manicured are now in disrepair and unkempt. Many of the houses on my block are vacant and boarded up, but the old vacant lot is still there. As I parked in front of it, for a few minutes, a thousand memories raced through my mind.

I remember a particular kid on our street that always came to the lot to play ball with us. He usually had his black high top canvas tennis shoes tied only halfway up, and there were always two or three empty eyelets at the tops of his shoes. He was one of the most impatient kids I ever knew. When his shoelaces became knotted, he never took time to sit down and patiently untie them. He just took a pocketknife and cut off the knot; thus his shoes were always only laced halfway.

I thought about him recently as I read and studied Nehemiah Chapter Five. I came to this conclusion. Rebuilders never cut what they can untie! They work through the knots of interpersonal relationships without cutting them off. They untie them so they can be tied again the next morning. Think about it. Rebuilders never cut what they can untie.

Conflict resolution is a hot topic in the business world and social arena today. It should be. Conflict can tear your team apart, whether you are on the court, in the home, at the office, or in the church. Conflict can do irreparable damage. Wherever you find two or more people, you often find the need for effective conflict resolution. Disagreements are inevitable. Some men and women lose their jobs because they never learn the secrets of conflict resolution. They simply go through life cutting what they could untie. Some churches split because they never understand the secrets of conflict resolution. Some homes break up. Why? Because too many husbands and wives cut what they could untie.

When we come to Nehemiah Chapter Five, we find him faced with the real possibility that the rebuilding of the walls will not be completed, due to conflict among members of his own team. The manner in which we learn to resolve our conflicts will go a long way in determining the success of our own personal rebuilding projects. We might do everything else right. We might get started right; we might build a team spirit; we might let go without letting up; we might know the importance of overcoming our obstacles. However, if we do not learn the secrets of conflict resolution, we will never see the job of rebuilding completed.

Some people never rebuild relationships, because when conflict comes, they simply cut the knot instead of taking time to untie it. Relationships, like shoelaces, can be retied to the top again if they are not severed. If we have any hope of rebuilding, we must avoid the temptation to simply take out a pocketknife and cut the knot. Rebuilders know the importance of never cutting what they can untie. When tensions build up and relationships become tied in knots, our general tendency is to simply cut the knots off. It takes patience and determination to untie a tense situation. This is exactly what we find Nehemiah doing in Chapter Five.

Our story unfolds in the early verses of the chapter when the people stop their work and get into conflict with one another regarding their personal dealings. They were rebuilding the wall, and at the same time, creating invisible walls between themselves. Nehemiah was faced with a situation that could easily get out of hand and deter the work of rebuilding the walls. A conflict arose among the Jews that was precipitated by a famine (Neh. 5:3). Men and women had mortgaged their homes to get food. Taxes were choking the life out of them (Neh. 5:4). If that were not bad enough, their own Jewish brothers were ripping them off with outlandish interest rates. The situation was so bleak that some were even selling their children into slavery. Is it any wonder that Nehemiah became "very angry?" (Neh. 5:6). This called for someone skilled in conflict resolution, or the ultimate goal of seeing the walls rebuilt would never be accomplished. It was a strategic time in the rebuilding process.

Nehemiah knew that if he was going to get the walls rebuilt he could not cut what he could untie. In the remaining verses of the chapter, we watch this skilled rebuilder begin to untie the knots of conflict and resolve the problems so everyone could go back to work. We ultimately read that "the wall was finished in 52 days" (Neh. 6:15).

Rebuilders never cut what they can untie. While this part of our volume does not report to be an exhaustive treatise on conflict resolution, we learn from Nehemiah some valuable principles that when put into practice can bring about the same results in our own personal experience. Nehemiah is saying to us that in conflict resolution there is a time to back off. There is a time to stand up. There is a time to give in. There is a time to reach out. Rebuilders never cut what they can untie because they know...*it's never too late for a new beginning.*

Chapter Nineteen

There is a time to back off

IRONICALLY, Nehemiah began the process of conflict resolution by backing off. Why? One reason. "I became very angry" (Neh. 5:6). We are talking about justified righteous indignation here. Nehemiah was still wise enough to know that in conflict resolution there are times when the best thing we can do is back off and give some "serious thought" to the situation (Neh. 5:7).

Nehemiah's response to conflict among his friends was "anger." He admitted it. In fact, he wrote it down in his memoirs for all to read centuries later. He did not try to conceal it. He did not excuse it. He did not minimize it. He did not act as if it were not there. He did not couch it in "legalese" or different types of technicalities. And, he did not try to repress it. He admitted it! He said, "I became very angry" (Neh. 5:6).

What made Nehemiah so angry? He knew his people were doing something in diametric opposition to the plain teaching of scripture. The Jewish Torah taught those people that "if you lend money to my people who are poor you shall not charge him interest" (Lev. 25:35-40). "To your brother you shall not charge interest, that the Lord your God may bless you in all to which you set your hand" (Deut. 23:20). Nehemiah became angry because the people knowingly and blatantly were disobeying God's clear teaching.

Nehemiah openly and honestly admits his anger. Many conflicts are never resolved because we are busy trying to excuse our anger. Some say, "Well, I'm just redheaded." Or, "I'm Irish!" Others say, "Well, that's simply my temperament. My dad was like that and I got it from him." We have all sorts of convenient little ways to avoid responsibility and project blame for our anger onto parents, friends, and sometimes even to God himself. And we wonder why we live with so much unresolved conflict.

Some conflicts are never resolved because we seek to justify our anger. We are quick to say, "You make me act like that. You know where my hot button is and you push it!" We avoid responsibility by implying it's someone else's fault. Some simply repress their anger. Thus, like a cancer it eats away at them. Nehemiah did none of these things. He freely admitted his anger. There was no doubt about it. But he immediately did a wise thing that eventually ended in conflict resolution. He backed off. He gave "serious thought" to the circumstance and situation (Neh. 5:7). Many conflicts today are never resolved because we will not back off. Instead, we barge in with our anger and agitate the situation that much more. In short, we cut what we could untie. Some of us go right from "anger" in Nehemiah 5:6, to the "rebuke" in Nehemiah 5:7, without making a stop at that important phrase in between – "after serious thought." In conflict resolution, there is a time to back off. Many conflicts are never resolved because good people have not learned this, and when anger arises they do not realize that it is time to back off.

Note what Nehemiah did. He gave it "serious thought." This phrase translates two Hebrew words, one meaning "to counsel, or to give advice," and the other meaning "the inner man." This word is translated "heart" over 500 times in the Old Testament. Nehemiah was literally saying, "I backed off and listened to my heart. I counseled with myself." It is a very wise thing to back off and listen to our heart, as Nehemiah was doing when conflicts arose. Instead of speaking first in anger, we would be much better off if we would back off and listen to our own heart for a while.

This is a vital and important step in conflict resolution. We find it throughout the Bible. It is exactly what Habakkuk did in Chapter One of the Book that bears his name. He was frustrated and angry with God. In the early verses of Chapter Two, we find him climbing up in a watchtower to "wait to see what God will say to me." Habakkuk knew the principle of backing off and listening to his heart in conflict resolution. Have you ever been tempted to write a letter in anger? Don't do it. Back off and listen to your heart. Wait a couple of days. It will save you a lot of heartache, ill feelings, and difficult knots to untie in relationships along the way. In conflict resolution, there is a time to back off.

Nehemiah was giving himself some time to get things in proper perspective. In the process of backing off, he decided on a course of action so that his people could get back to the ultimate task of rebuilding the walls. Nehemiah never lost sight of his ultimate goal and purpose. Too often in our anger we shoot from the hip, and fail in attempts to resolve conflicts.

We fail to realize there is a time to back off.

Rebuilders never cut what they can untie. They realize early on that there is a time to back off and listen to their heart. They do not skip the phrase, "serious thought," between being angry and rebuking someone else. There is a time to back off. *It's never too late for a new beginning.*

Chapter Twenty

There is a time to stand up

NEHEMIAH acknowledged that there is a time to back off. He now declares there is also a time to stand up. He boldly confronts those he believed to be in the wrong. "I rebuked the nobles and rulers, and said to them, 'Each of you is exacting usury from his brother.' So I called a great assembly against them. Then I said, 'What you are doing is not good. Should you not walk in the fear of our God, because of the reproach of the nations, our enemies?'" (Neh. 5:7, 9). Nehemiah had the courage to stand up and take the needed action. He "rebuked" the nobles and elders, and brought them face to face with the real issue. The issue was, in their charging interest rates to their own Jewish brothers, they had become a reproach to God in the eyes of those around them (Neh. 5:9).

Conflict resolution does not mean giving in at all costs. It does not mean to simply back off all the time. Nehemiah was a strong leader. He stood up for what was right. He rebuked those who were in the wrong. Conflict resolution is not simply another form of pacifism. Sometimes we have to "make peace." On a Galilean hillside one day, Jesus pronounced a blessing on the "peacemakers," not the "peace lovers." Here we see Nehemiah patiently untying what some would have hastily cut. In resolving conflict, he is showing us that there is a time to back off, but there is also a time to stand up.

After we back off and think through the situation, many of us never resolve conflicts because we lack the courage to confront. We settle down and pacify ourselves with 100 reasons to simply do nothing. How many conflicts are involved with readers of this volume that have never been resolved? Is it because someone simply backed off and left it at that? Conflicts are resolved when we realize there is a time to stand up.

Some never resolve conflicts in the home because they never deal with the real issues. They back off, but they don't stand up. Therefore, like a boil that continues to fester, the relationship continues to sour. There are others who stand up quite frequently, but do not know the principle of backing off, and thus speak in anger and only complicate the matter. There is definitely a time to stand up, but Nehemiah is showing us it should always follow a time when we back off. Rebuilders never cut what they can untie because they know…*it's never too late for a new beginning.*

Chapter Twenty-one

There is a time to give in

NEHEMIAH reminds us not only is there a time to back off and a time to stand up, but there is also a time to give in. Hear him as he challenges his Jewish brothers. Listen even to the conciliatory tone of his voice. Can you hear it? I think I can. He is saying to them, "Give in." In his words, "I also, with my brethren and my servants, am lending them money and grain. Please, let us stop this usury! Restore now to them, even this day, their lands, their vineyards, their olive groves, and their houses, also a hundredth of the money and the grain, the new wine and the oil, that you have charged them" (Neh. 5:10-11). This is Nehemiah's way of reminding his people there is a time to give in. He's letting them know they will be better off for it. He frequently uses "we" and "us," and, in so doing, identifies with his people. "Let us stop this usury. Let us restore the vineyards." There is a time to give in.

Nehemiah is not showing weakness here. He is showing true strength. In fact, it takes more security to give in than it does to stand up. Almost anyone can stand up. But those who resolve conflicts know there is a time to give in. There is a time to allow the other person to save face in the process of conflict resolution. Some of us only want to take in relationships. There are times when giving in on nonessentials is not a dirty word. There are times when it's better to lose a few little battles so we can still win the big war.

This very principle is what happened in the sixth chapter of the New Testament Book of Acts when the ministry of the deacon was born. If Nehemiah 5 is a wonderfully instructive chapter in the Old Testament on conflict resolution, then Acts 6 is its parallel in the New Testament. In the early church, the Hellenistic Jews (those with Greek backgrounds) felt the apostles, who in their minds were favoring the Hebraic Jews, were slighting them. A conflict arose. Dissension came to the early church. People were about to leave the building for the battle. What did the apostles do to resolve the conflict? They knew there was a time to back off, and thus they did. Then there was a time to stand up and a time to give in. They appointed seven deacons to minister to the early church. Interestingly, when we read their seven names recorded in Acts 6, every one of them had Hellenistic names. What a beautiful example of conflict resolution. They knew the principle of never cutting what they could untie. So, skillfully, and delicately, with great determination, they untied the knot of the problem. The conflict was resolved, and the Word of God spread. Why? Because they were wise enough to know there was a time to give in.

Let's return to Nehemiah. We find him doing what he has been his whole story. He is leading by example. He never asks his people to do anything he does not do himself. If it is to work diligently upon the wall, he is right there with them. If it is to pray, he is the first one on his knees. If it is to work overtime, he is the last one to leave. He constantly leads by example. Now, he is asking them to do the right thing for those among them who are underprivileged. And once again he leads the way (Neh. 5:10). Being an example ourselves is vitally important in conflict resolution, whether it is in the home, in the office, in the social arena, or wherever.

Nehemiah is the master at conflict resolution. We get a glimpse of how he gives in (Neh. 5:14-19). He knew that nothing was more important than completing the rebuilding of the walls and hanging the gates of Jerusalem. Therefore, he was wise enough to know there was not only a time to back off, and a time to stand up, but also a time to give in.

What is more important in parenting, Dad? To see that the wall is completed and that boy or girl matures with values, and convictions, and commitments? Or is it more important to be able to say that you won every argument, and kept them under your thumb? You must know when to stand up, but also know when to give in. Learn when to lose a few little battles on nonessentials so that you can win the ultimate war. What is more important to you as a wife? Seeing the wall completed, or being able to say, "I told you so." There is a time to give in. And the time to give in is not a sign of weakness, but of strength. Some of us never resolve conflicts because we never give in. We are always insisting on winning every argument. We always want to have our own way.

Rebuilders never cut what they can untie. They know there is a time to back off, a time to stand up, but also a time to give in. They also know…*it's never too late for a new beginning.*

Chapter Twenty-two

There is a time to reach out

ONCE again, as we come to Nehemiah 5:10-13, we find him using personal pronouns such as "we," "us," etc. Hear him as he pleads, "Please, let us stop this usury!" (Neh. 5:10). He is reaching out to them. He is building bridges to walk across in order to resolve conflicts and relationships. Here is a vital principle in conflict resolution. Nehemiah is building consensus.

There is a sense of urgency as he reaches out. He says, "Restore now...even this day" (Neh. 5:11). He didn't tell them to go home and think about it. No. This was a time to reach out. Do it now. It's the right thing to do! Yes, Nehemiah was conciliatory. He backed off, stood up, and gave in, and now he is reaching out. He is conciliatory without compromising his position. He was a man whose character and integrity was beyond question. He did not lower his own standards to resolve conflict. He reached out to those nobles and elders to join him in doing what was right. Nehemiah was following what would be Christ's own formula for conflict resolution. It is found in Matthew 18:15-16. First, Nehemiah confronts his offenders in private. He says, "I told them" (Neh. 5:7). When the response was not positive, he moved to a more public confrontation in Nehemiah 5:12.

What was the result of Nehemiah's backing off, standing up, giving in, and reaching out? Nehemiah 5:13 records, "And all the assembly said, 'Amen!' and praised the Lord! Then the people did according to this promise." Let the amen sound from his people again! Shalom returned. Now, that is what we call conflict resolution.

Do you need a good biblical illustration of this in the New Testament? Turn to the little Book of Philemon, tucked away near the end of your New Testament. Paul wrote the book on conflict resolution in his letter to Philemon. The whole story is of a conflict between Philemon and a man by the name of Onesimus. In his letter to Philemon, Paul says in essence that there is a time to back off. He reminds Philemon that he "makes mention of him often in his prayers" (Phil. 4). Then Paul reveals that there is a time to stand up. He confronts Philemon by saying, "If you count me as a partner, receive Onesimus back as you would me" (Phil. 17). Next, Paul says there is a time to give in. He continues, "If he has wronged you, or owes you anything, put it on my account. I will repay it" (Phil. 18). And then he reaches out to his friend Philemon. He says, "Having confidence in your obedience, I write to you, knowing that you will do even more than I say" (Phil. 21). These principles work. They worked in the Bible and they work today. They work in the home. They work in the office. They work in the social arena. They work anywhere conflict arises.

Rebuilders never cut what they can untie. Do you need an Old Testament illustration? You need look no further than the initial book of the Bible, the Book of Genesis, and the story of Joseph. Talk about someone in need of conflict resolution with his own family. Jealousy, lying, and conflict ripped his family apart and separated them for many years. We recall that Joseph was eventually sold into slavery in Egypt. Through a miraculous set of events, in his young adulthood he ultimately became the Prime Minister of Egypt. A famine came to Israel. His brothers, who had betrayed him, came to Egypt unknowing of Joseph's circumstances. They came to Egypt to try to find food. One of the most moving scenes in the entire Bible is when the conflict is resolved between Joseph and his brothers. What did Joseph do? First, he backed off. Before he met them, he got alone and wept. Then he stood up. He came to them, confronted them, and exclaimed, "I am your brother!" Next, he gave in. Finally he reached out. He came to them, and they fell into each other's arms and kissed. Joseph was one of the first to know that rebuilders never cut what they can untie.

The entire Bible is a textbook on conflict resolution. Our Lord Jesus, Himself, had to deal with conflict on most every page of the Gospels. In the Book of Mark alone, we find others in conflict with Him on 26 different occasions. There was conflict in Nazareth. There was conflict with His friends. There was conflict with His family. There was conflict with the Pharisees. There was conflict with the disciples. There was conflict with Judas. There was conflict with Simon Peter. The Bible is the most relevant book to be found anywhere, if we would just read it and put it into practice at the point of our need.

Now, how are you going to resolve conflict in your home? Some stand up before they back off. Thus, they speak in anger and drive a wedge deeper into the broken relationship. Others give in before they stand up. Thus, they lose their authority in the home. How many parents find themselves at this particular place in conflict with their own children? That is, they give in time and time again without ever standing up to them. There is a proper pattern at work here. There is a time to back off. Then a time to stand up. Then a time to give in.

Finally, there is a time to reach out. This is a time for all of us who are interested in conflict resolution to reach out to one another. We can begin by following the biblical pattern, and stop cutting what we could be untying.

Some of us attempt to deal with conflict by employing only the first step. We simply back off, and that is it. We never stand up. We never give in. We never reach out. When we play the conflict resolution game like that, we play what some call "lose-lose" in relationships. Had Nehemiah only backed off, he would have lost, and all the Jews would have lost at the same time, because the walls would never have been completed.

Others attempt to play the conflict resolution game by employing only the second step. That is, all they do is stand up. When you play this, you play what some call "win-lose" in relationships. This is a dead-end street. Some only have relationships if they win every single argument. Had Nehemiah played this way, the walls would never have been completed.

There are still others who play the conflict resolution game with only the third step. They never stand up. They never back off. They simply give in time and time again, playing what is called "lose-win" in the relationship. Thus, they receive no respect from others, and think they can only have a relationship as long as they always let the other person win. Had Nehemiah played this way, the walls would never have been completed. There is a time for backing off, but there is also a time for standing up, giving in, and reaching out. When we put them all into practice in the proper pattern, we learn, like Nehemiah, to resolve conflicts, and end up in a "win-win" relationship. Rebuilders never cut what they can untie. Like Nehemiah, they keep their focus on the rebuilt wall.

Think about our Lord Jesus Christ. You were in conflict with Him in His purpose and plan for your life. The Bible reminds us that all of us have gone our own way and done our own thing. So what did He do to resolve conflict? He put all four of these principles into play. He backed off. Can you see Him in Gethsemane's garden in "serious thought and prayer?" He backed off and took counsel with His heart. "Father, if it is Your will, take this cup away from Me; nevertheless not My will, but Yours, be done" (Luke 22:42). Yes, He too knew there was a time to back off.

Next, our Lord knew there was a time to stand up. Can you see Him before Caiaphas, before Herod, before Pontius Pilate, before all of His accusers? When asked, "Are You then the Son of God?" He simply replied, "You rightly say that I am." (Luke 22:70). He stood up.

Then, He gave in. He had a goal in mind to build the wall of a broken relationship with you. Thus, He not only backed off and stood up, He gave in. No one dragged Him to Calvary. No one pushed Him up the Via Dolorosa. He willingly laid down His life like a lamb to the slaughter. He gave in.

And, finally He reached out. Do you see Him on the cross? His arms are outstretched, reaching out to you. He died your death so you could live His life. He took your sin so you could take His righteousness. He reached out on the cross to resolve conflict with you and me.

Talk about conflict resolution; the Lord Jesus is the

epitome of it. In fact, He wrote the book on it. He calls upon us to be reconciled to God.

You and I do not have to go through life like that kid on my block that played with us on the old vacant lot. You don't have to wear your shoes only laced up halfway because you have continually cut the knots of interpersonal relationships. When you cut your shoelaces, it simply means you cannot tie them to the top again. Rebuilders, like Nehemiah, never cut what they can untie. They know...*it's never too late for a new beginning!*

Part VI

Rebuilders finish strong

TWO of the most respected men in the evangelical world during our lifetime have been Billy Graham and Chuck Colson. Billy Graham is a man whose entire life has been identified with integrity and character. After over half a century in the public eye, he has never gotten off on a side street or on the sideline. On the other hand, Chuck Colson is a man whose walls came crashing down. Here is a man who wandered off onto some side streets, and for a while was put on the sideline in prison. However, he is a man who came back and rebuilt his broken life. What do Billy Graham and Chuck Colson have in common? They are both finishing strong. As Nehemiah has walked us through the principles of rebuilding, we now finally see that rebuilders are those who finish strong.

We have all heard of Billy Graham. He started his ministry in the mid-1940's, and at the age of 27 began to gather crowds in his preaching services. However, has anyone heard of Chuck Templeton or Bron Clifford? In William Martin's biography of Billy Graham, he says that Chuck Templeton was "the most gifted and talented young preacher of his era." Billy Graham,

Chuck Templeton, and Bron Clifford were all young preachers of renown in the mid-1940's. Many authors have recounted their stories, but none better than my friend Steve Farrar in his recent volume entitled *Finishing Strong*. In 1946, the National Association of Evangelicals published an article entitled, *The Best Used Men of God*. The article highlighted Chuck Templeton and made no mention of Billy Graham. When Bron Clifford was 25 years of age, he was preaching to thousands of people. Everywhere he went there were overflow crowds. It is reported that by the age of 25, he had touched more lives and set more attendance records than any clergyman in American history. He was tall and handsome, intelligent and eloquent. In fact, he had opportunities from Hollywood producers to play significant parts in many of the Biblical movies that emerged in the late 40's and early 50's.

Yes, we have heard of Billy Graham, but whatever became of Chuck Templeton and Bron Clifford? Chuck Templeton left the ministry to pursue a journalistic career, and by 1950 was reported to no longer believe in the Lord Jesus Christ, in what one might call the orthodox sense. In 1954, Bron Clifford lost his health and family, and became an alcoholic. At the age of 35, this great preacher died in a rundown hotel room on the outskirts of Amarillo, Texas, of cirrhosis of the liver.

Rebuilders finish strong. Chuck Colson is a rebuilder. His walls fell down. His gates were burned. He crashed in the Watergate fiasco. He got on a side street, and was put on a sideline. However, he came out of prison and began to rebuild his life. He got started right. He built a team spirit. He let go without letting up in prison ministries all over the world. He overcame his obstacles. He never cut what he could untie and today he is finishing strong.

As we open our Bibles to Nehemiah Chapter Six, it is important that we remember we are talking about the rebuilding process. Many are rebuilding that which has been broken. In Chapter Six, it was a long way from that day in Persia when he heard the first report of the broken walls and burned gates. It has been a long way from that midnight ride he took in Chapter Two when he reviewed the ruins by himself in the middle of the darkness of the night. We passed the halfway mark in Nehemiah 4:6 when the walls were half completed. We are headed down the back stretch. We can see the finish line. The walls are up. All that's left to do is hang the gates (Neh. 6:1). We find Nehemiah here on the last lap of his race, and he's reminding us that rebuilders finish strong. They sprint the last lap. He encourages us today to keep running so that we might make it to Nehemiah 6:15: "So the wall was finished in fifty-two days." There is so much behind those words in this verse. We would never have arrived here with Nehemiah had he not stopped in Chapter One to show us that rebuilders get started right. He made an honest evaluation. He identified with the need. He took personal responsibility. And he moved out of his comfort zone.

We may never have gotten to Nehemiah 6:15 where the walls were finished had Nehemiah not stopped in Chapter Two to show us the importance of building a team spirit. He started with his goal in mind. He seized his opportunities. He made a careful analysis of his situation. He motivated his people to get off dead center. And he stayed on track.

We may have never made it to Nehemiah 6:15 had Nehemiah not stopped in Chapter Three to remind us that rebuilders let go without letting up. They know it's more important to delegate than to dictate or abdicate. He set clear objectives with specific tasks. He picked the right person for the right job. He was an example himself. He held his people accountable, and he gave a genuine pat on the back.

We may never have made it to Nehemiah 6:15 had Nehemiah not stopped for a moment in Chapter Four to remind us that in rebuilding it is the "YAC" that matters most. He overcame his obstacles. He knew it was the "yards after contact" that really mattered. He dealt with conflict head-on. He made proper adjustments. He kept doing what was right, and he rallied his troops.

Finally, we might never have gotten to Nehemiah 6:15 had we not learned the important lesson in Chapter Five that rebuilders never cut what they can untie. They resolve their conflicts. How? They know there is a time to back off. There is a time to stand up. There is a time to give in. And there is a time to reach out.

Now, after all this, Nehemiah heads down the back stretch. His goal is in sight. The finish line. Mission accomplished. Nehemiah 6:15 – "The walls were completed!" Some of us are at this point of rebuilding in our own personal journeys. Nehemiah is shouting to us today that rebuilders finish strong.

The last lap is often the most dangerous time of the whole rebuilding process. I know men and women who have gone through all the principles we have seen outlined in five chapters, yet quit when the goal was in sight. The enemy comes along and makes one final ditch attempt to keep Nehemiah from the finish line. The enemy sought to get him on the side street and when that didn't work, they tried to get him on the sideline. Nehemiah asked two questions in Chapter Six that formed the basis of his successful finish. When tempted to get on the side streets, he kept focused and asked, "Why should the work cease while I leave it and go down to you?" (Neh. 6:3). When he was tempted to get on the sideline, he kept faithful and asked, "Should such a man as I flee?" (Neh. 6:11). These are the two questions each of us must ask as we too finish our own particular race. Of all the wonderful things that can be said and written about Nehemiah, this is at the top of the list. He teaches us how to finish strong. After all, isn't that what is important? It's not so much how long our race may be, or even how difficult, but how we finish.

Nehemiah's goal was in sight. The walls were rebuilt. All that was left to do was hang the gates. He was on the last lap of a long and difficult race, over all types of hills and valleys. He was the original triathlete. Now he can see the finish line ahead. As he sprints for the tape, he shouts two very important principles to us that seem to keep echoing down through the corridors of the centuries. Can you hear him? "Stay off the side streets – keep focused!" "Stay off the sidelines – keep faithful!" Nehemiah's concern for you and me is that it also might be said of us that "our walls were completed." Yes, *it's never too late for a new beginning.*

Chapter Twenty-three

Stay off the side streets — keep focused

THE STORY unfolds with Nehemiah's old nemesis, Sanballat, and his deceitful friends, hearing that Nehemiah had rebuilt the wall and all that was left to do was hang the gates. They made one final attempt to derail him. "Come, let us meet on the plain of Ono," they requested. They wanted Nehemiah to meet them halfway. They tried to trick Nehemiah with his own game. He had just been talking about the importance of conflict resolution. Now they are saying, "Let's sit down." "Let's come down to the plain of Ono." "Come on, Nehemiah, give in and reach out." Nehemiah was wise enough to know this was not the time to give in or reach out, but the time to stand up and finish the wall.

Often, when our own wall is virtually completed, and our task is almost done, we think we are home free. We are tempted to let up, and then some Sanballat comes along, enticing us to get on a side street, to come down to the plain of Ono. Nehemiah responded with the first of two questions in Chapter Six – "I am doing a great work, so that I cannot come down. Why should the work cease while I leave it and go down to you?" (Neh. 6:3). But, they persisted. "They sent me this message four times, and I answered them in the same manner" (Neh. 6:4). Nehemiah kept the answer "in the same manner," and continued to reply that he was doing a great work, and he would not come down.

A fifth time they sent "an open letter." They said, "It is reported among the nations, and Geshem says, that you and the Jews plan to rebel; therefore, according to these rumors, you are rebuilding the wall, that you may be their King" (Neh. 6:6). "It is reported." That is, "they" say. Who is "they?" Rumors have two distinguishing characteristics. Rumors are nameless. Have you ever noticed how the source of a rumor is never quoted? Why? There is not one! Rumors are not only nameless; they are shameless and often exaggerated. In this case, they were exaggerating the rumor to say that Nehemiah wanted to be the king of Judah. All this was an attempt to get Nehemiah on a side street before the walls were completed. They were attempting to get him to leave the building to come down to the plain of Ono and get on a side street. Note that Nehemiah stayed off the side streets by keeping focused.

What should be your response when confronted with nameless, shameless rumors? Have you ever been the brunt of a rumor? Think about it. It was nameless and shameless. Nehemiah teaches us what to do with rumors. Note his reply, "No such things as you say are being done, but you invent them in your own heart...Now therefore, O God, strengthen my hands" (Neh. 6:8-9). Nehemiah dealt with the rumor in three distinct ways. He refuted it; he rebuked it; he referred it. What should we do with rumors? First, refute it.

Nehemiah said, "No such things as you say are being done." (Neh. 6:8). Next, rebuke it. He went on to say, "You invent them in your own heart." (Neh. 6:8). Then, refer it. Nehemiah simply referred it to the Lord and went on about his business, keeping focused. He said, "Now therefore, O God, strengthen my hands" (Neh. 6:9). That's good advice for any of us who are the brunt of rumors. Refute it. Rebuke it. Refer it to the Lord, and go on. Rebuilders stay off the side streets. They keep focused.

What is Ono? It is a side street. There is nothing necessarily wrong with it. We have all been down side streets at one time or another in our lives. When our children were small, we made investments of our time and resources by buying them memories on family vacations. One summer, we took a car trip from Fort Lauderdale to the nation's capital. It took us more than a day to simply get out of Florida. The Fort Lauderdale/Miami area is hundreds of miles from the Florida/Georgia border! On the second day, we were winding our way through the mountains of North Carolina and Virginia. Having stopped for gasoline, I saw on the map a road that looked like a wonderful shortcut that would cut off scores of miles to our destination. I took that side street. What I didn't know was that most of it was a two-lane road, up and over, and around and through some of the most rugged mountains I have ever seen. What I thought was a shortcut ended up adding several hours to our trip, not to mention a lot of conversation along the way. Side streets!

I pastored in Fort Lauderdale, Florida, for 15 years. This city is called the "Venice of America", as there are over 200 miles of waterways inside the city limits. There are hundreds of homes on the canals; water taxis are the way of transportation.

Street after street ends at a canal. It took me awhile to learn that if I was ever going to get anywhere I had to stay on the main streets. Every time I would try to beat the traffic by getting on a side street, I would end up at a dead end, a cul-de-sac, a circle, or a canal. If you and I are going to rebuild, we have to learn the lessons of staying off the side streets and keeping focused. Ono may be *good*, but *good* is the enemy of the best.

What can keep us off the side street? Focus. It is possible to do everything else right, then get on a side street before our task is completed. I have seen this happen in marriages, in relationships, in churches, and in businesses. Have you ever been on a side street? When you are in the process of rebuilding a marriage, some Sanballat or Tobiah can come along and get you on a side street. There are those who will try anything to get you off the main road of rebuilding. Some who are rebuilding relationships get off on side streets. Some who are seeking to rebuild their vocational life are prone to take side streets. Rebuilders finish strong. How? They stay off the side streets and remain focused on what they are to do.

Nehemiah was focused. Listen to his response. "I am doing a great work, so that I cannot come down. Why should the work cease while I leave it and go down to you?" (Neh. 6:3). He saw what he was doing as a "great work." Lack of focus is often the problem in rebuilding. This is especially true when we are nearing the finish line. We live in a day when some moms and dads do not see that raising children is a "great work." So often in the process of rebuilding we take a little side trip to Ono, get on a side street, and lose our focus.

Is anyone reading these words today with the rebuilding project almost finished? Your walls are up, and all that's left to do is hang the gates. Perhaps a marriage, a relationship, the rebuilding of self-confidence, finds your walls almost completed. This is one of the most dangerous times in all the rebuilding process. Nehemiah shouts a warning to all of us today. Stay off the side streets – keep focused. Join him in seeing that what you are doing is a great work and you cannot come down. Rebuilders finish strong because they know...*it's never too late for a new beginning.*

Chapter Twenty-four

Stay off the sidelines — keep faithful

ANYONE who has ever played on an athletic team does not like to be on the sidelines. I was on the sidelines with my friend, Mike Ditka, in December of 1998, as he coached the New Orleans Saints to that memorable 22-3 victory over the Dallas Cowboys. As I rubbed shoulders that day with those massive athletes, the thing that interested me the most was how much those who were on the sidelines wanted to be in the game. Anyone who has ever aspired to be an actor or an actress doesn't like to be "in the wings or on the sidelines" when the action is on center stage. Rebuilders finish strong because they stay off the sidelines and keep faithful.

The apex of my own athletic career occurred decades ago in the East Side Little League in Fort Worth, Texas. We played our games at the old Del Murray Field, and I played for the Rox-ex Exterminating Company Tigers. I can still feel those old gray flannel uniforms with the orange trim. My little league coach was a man by the name of Jerry Peden.

He was a big guy. I was 10 years of age, and most of my teammates were 11 and 12. At every practice, Mr. Peden would drill into our minds these words, "Don't get called out on strikes." He wanted us to know that if we were going to strike out that he wanted us to go down swinging. In others words, he did not want us to stand there with the bat on our shoulder and watch the third strike go by without swinging at it. Whenever I would be at bat and get two strikes, I would look down the third base line where Mr. Peden was in the coaching box. He would lock his eyes on me, cup his hands around his mouth, and shout those words to me, "Don't get called out on strikes!" Even as I type these words on my computer, I can still feel the fear I used to know in hearing Mr. Peden say those words.

By the time Nehemiah gets to Chapter Six, he has overcome all sorts of obstacles. There was opposition from without – *strike one*. There was opposition from within – *strike two*. Just before he hits his homerun in Nehemiah 6:15 when the walls are completed, the enemy throws him a curve ball. His adversaries say, "Let us meet together in the house of God, within the temple" (Neh. 6:10). Had he done so, it would have put Nehemiah on the sidelines for the rest of his life, but he was too wise to get called out on strikes. He was focused. He was faithful.

The enemy sought to entice Nehemiah to meet with them "within the temple." This adversary was not simply trying to get him on a side street, but completely on the sidelines. He called Nehemiah to meet not just at the temple, but "within" the temple, that is, the Holy Place. The same word is used here that is used in I Samuel 6:1 to describe how Isaiah's vision of God saw His robe filling the temple. In Ezekiel 41:4, this is the same word that describes "The Most Holy Place." In II

Chronicles 26, Uzziah went into the temple. Remember, only the priests were allowed to go there. Even King Uzziah had been warned not to do so. Do you remember the result when he entered the temple? He was fortunate to escape with his life, but he contracted leprosy. Nehemiah was a layman. This was nothing more than a blatant attempt to put Nehemiah on the sidelines just before the walls were completed and the gates were hung. It was an enticement to do that which was contrary to the plain teaching of the Word so that the judgment of God would come down upon him.

What do we see here? We see a man who lived his life under the authority of the Word of God. He knew the Bible said he was not to go within the temple, and thus he submitted to the Word of God and the God of the Word. He says to us today, "Stay off the sidelines – keep faithful."

Once again, Nehemiah responded with a question, "And I said, 'Should such a man as I flee?'" (Neh. 6:11). If Ono was a side street, going within the temple was the sideline. I know a lot of men and women who have gotten started right, yet when they came to the last lap they were put on the sideline because they tried to finish the job without keeping faithful. I know a lot of my own peers in ministry who lost focus and got off on a side street somewhere. It was not long before they had lost their faithfulness and were put on the sidelines.

Listen to Nehemiah, "Should such a man as I flee?" We live in a day where we find a lot of fleeing people who simply run out on life and on their opportunities. There are many people who take side streets that lead to the sidelines. Escapism takes all kinds of forms. Some who are rebuilding relationships often find it easier to simply flee before they finish the job. They just leave. More and more of those who are building walls in ministry get on the side streets, and end up fleeing. Some who are in the process of rebuilding their marriages invest years and years of their lives building a wall, only to flee when the task is almost completed.

The Psalmist felt this. He said, "Oh, that I had wings like a dove! I would fly away and be at rest" (Ps. 55:6). Some of us identify with this. Perhaps someone is reading these words who is saying, "Oh that I had the wings of a dove and then I would fly off and be at rest." Guess what? You don't have any wings! You can't fly off. You can't run out on life every time things don't go your way. You can't flee. You can't quit. "Should such a man as I flee?"

This is exactly what our Lord was getting at when He said, "No one, having put his hand to the plow, and looking back, is fit for the kingdom of God" (Luke 9:62). More and more young couples are approaching the wedding altar today saying that if things don't meet their expectations they'll just quit. No. Marriage is a life commitment.

Is anyone reading these words that is about to quit, about to flee? You have worked so hard to get the wall up; you have seen so much accomplished, and yet you are tempted to flee. Listen, you must join Nehemiah in saying, "Should such a man as I flee?" Stay off the side streets – keep focused. Stay off the sidelines – keep faithful.

In rebuilding, it's how we finish that's important. Nehemiah had his Sanballat and Tobiah. The Lord Jesus had His Judas. We all have someone who may try to get us on a side street or even on a sideline. Nehemiah is not speaking softly here. He is shouting to those of us who are approaching the finish line, "Stay off the side streets – keep focused. Stay off the sidelines – keep faithful."

"So the wall was finished" (Neh. 6:15). That may be the biggest understatement in the book. Nehemiah had come to Jerusalem with a single focused objective, to rebuild the walls. He began with a goal in mind. He stayed off the side streets – he kept focused. He stayed off the sidelines – he kept faithful. And thus we read, "So the wall was finished on the twenty-fifth day of Elul, in fifty-two days" (Neh. 6:15). We may have never read these words had Nehemiah not run the race as he did. Now, he's showing us the importance of finishing what we started. Like the shepherd who kept focused "until he found the lost sheep," Nehemiah keeps moving toward his goal. What is it that you have started to rebuild? Is it a marriage? Are you rebuilding after divorce? Are you rebuilding after the death of a loved one? Are you rebuilding a relationship? Are you rebuilding self-confidence? Are you rebuilding a church? Finish it. Finish it. "Should such a man as I flee?"

And what was the result when we read that the walls were completed? "And it happened, when all our enemies heard of it, and all the nations around us saw these things, that they were very disheartened in their own eyes; for they perceived that this work was done by our God." (Neh. 6:16). Nehemiah gave glory to God. God did it! Some of us who pray and trust Him while climbing up the ladder forget Him when we get to the top. Not Nehemiah! He gave glory to God.

Rebuilders finish strong. Think about it. Who generally wins the professional golf tournament? The one who finishes the strongest. The one who plays the final two or three holes with intensity, and passion, and skill. Even though the tournament consists of 72 holes, it's the last few that seem the most critical. Even if you hit the ball out of bounds back on hole number eight, you can still finish strong!

One of the great spectator sports is the Final Four of the college basketball playoffs. Who generally wins the NCAA tournament? The team that plays best in the final two minutes. It is the team that finishes strong who wins. Maybe you fouled out at a previous game. Get up. Get off the sidelines. Get back in the game. Stay off the side streets – keep focused. Stay off the sidelines – keep faithful. There is still time for you to see "the wall finished."

In the Olympics, the mile run is always a high-interest event. Even though the runners have been at it for the course of a mile, it generally comes down to the last 50 yards of the race. It is the one who finishes the strongest that generally wins. Perhaps you tripped and fell on an earlier lap around the track. Get up. Finish strong. Sprint the last lap. Keep focused, and keep faithful, so that your wall may be completed.

In the courtroom, who usually comes out on top? The opening arguments are important to set the direction. The examination and cross-examination of witnesses is vitally important. Jury selection is more and more vital in our present day, but often it is that final argument that leaves the most lasting impression with the jury. The attorney who finishes strongest is often the one who has the advantage.

And so it is in the rebuilding process in life. Whether we are rebuilding a home or a relationship, a marriage or a vocation, a church or a business, those who complete the job of rebuilding have a common characteristic. They finish strong. They sprint the last lap.

It is strange that if we get on a sideline, no matter how much good we might have done, we are generally remembered as one who *did not* finish strong. I have a lot of admiration for men and women in life who, for a while, might have lost focus or even faithfulness. For a while they might have gotten on a side street, or even off on the sideline, yet got back up and in the race. Because of certain circumstances or situations, some might even run with a slight limp while seeking to finish strong. We can all do this!

Perhaps someone is reading this volume that in a weak moment went down to the plain of Ono and met the enemy halfway. Perhaps you wish you could change the fact that you "ran into the temple." Perhaps you did that which was contrary to the Word of God. It's never too late for a new beginning. It's never too late to get back in the race. It's never too late to stay off the side streets and keep focused, to stay off the side streets and keep faithful.

What really matters is seeing "the wall completed." I think of John Mark in the Book of Acts. He finished strong! In fact, he gave us the gospel of Mark in our New Testament. But before he finished strong, he quit. He fled. He left Paul in a lurch on the first missionary journey. He got on a side street and eventually on the sideline for a while. However, he was encouraged by Barnabas. He got up, rejoined the race, and finished strong. I want to be a Barnabas, an encourager. Every time I read the Book of Mark, I am reminded that *it's never too late for a new beginning.*

Perhaps some that are reading this volume have fallen down on the track as you have run the race. Maybe you hit the ball out of bounds. Maybe you have gotten off main street onto a side street, but you are rebuilding! You can get up and get back in the race. What really matters now is how you finish the race. Don't get called out on strikes! Keep focused, and keep faithful, so that it might be said of you, "So the wall was finished." (Neh. 6:15) Nehemiah's two questions are pertinent and poignant for us today. "Why should the work cease while I leave it and go down to you?" Stay off the side streets – keep focused. "Should such a man as I flee?" Stay off the sidelines – keep faithful.

No one ever finished stronger than our Lord Jesus Christ. He is the epitome of One who got started right, who built a team spirit, who let go without letting up, who realized that "YAC" was what really mattered, and who never cut what He could untie. When His own finish line was in sight, He prayed, "I finished the work You gave Me to do" (John 17:4). The enemy tried to get Him on the side street. He took Him to a high mountain and tried to get Him to bow down. He took Him to the pinnacle of the temple and invited Him to jump off so that people would see Him for who He was. But He kept focused! Then, near the finish line, the enemy tried to get Him on the sidelines. The crowds jeered. They mocked. They spit. They screamed, "Come down if you are the Son of God." He could have called legions of angels to destroy the world and set Him free. Then, we hear Him echoing Nehemiah's own words, "I am doing a great work, so that I cannot come down. Why should the work cease while I leave it and go down to you?" (Neh. 6:3).

The Lord Jesus Christ kept focused and He kept faithful. He finished strong. And in the end, on the cross, He shouted, "It is finished!" To prove it, three days later He arose from the grave, the Living Lord and Savior.

I don't know about you, but I want to finish strong. I want to stay off the side streets, and keep focused. I want to stay off the sidelines, and keep faithful. Our Lord is standing at the finish line with arms outstretched. He is more interested in your rebuilding process than you are. He believes in you; do you believe in Him? Rebuilders finish strong because they know…*it's never too late for a new beginning.*

Appendix

Nehemiah

Nehemiah 1:1-11

Chapter 1

Nehemiah Prays for His People

¹The words of Nehemiah the son of Hachaliah. It came to pass in the month of Chislev, *in* the twentieth year, as I was in Shushan the citadel, ²that Hanani one of my brethren came with men from Judah; and I asked them concerning the Jews who had escaped, who had survived the captivity, and concerning Jerusalem. ³And they said to me, "The survivors who are left from the captivity in the province *are* there in great distress and reproach. The wall of Jerusalem is also broken down, and its gates *are* burned with fire."

⁴So it was, when I heard these words, that I sat down and wept, and mourned *for many* days; I was fasting and praying before the God of heaven. ⁵And I said: "I pray, LORD God of heaven, O great and awesome God, *You* who keep *Your* covenant and mercy with those who love You and observe Your commandments, ⁶"please let Your ear be attentive and Your eyes open, that You may hear the prayer of Your servant which I pray before You now, day and night, for the children of Israel Your servants, and confess the sins of the children of Israel which we have sinned against You. Both my father's

house and I have sinned. ⁷"We have acted very corruptly against You, and have not kept the commandments, the statutes, nor the ordinances which You commanded Your servant Moses. ⁸"Remember, I pray, the word that You commanded Your servant Moses, saying, '*If* you are unfaithful, I will scatter you among the nations; ⁹'but *if* you return to Me, and keep My commandments and do them, though some of you were cast out to the farthest part of the heavens, *yet* I will gather them from there, and bring them to the place which I have chosen as a dwelling for My name.' ¹⁰"Now these *are* Your servants and Your people, whom You have redeemed by Your great power, and by Your strong hand. ¹¹"O Lord, I pray, please let Your ear be attentive to the prayer of Your servant, and to the prayer of Your servants who desire to fear Your name; and let Your servant prosper this day, I pray, and grant him mercy in the sight of this man." For I was the king's cupbearer.

Nehemiah 2:1-20

Chapter 2

Nehemiah Sent to Judah

¹And it came to pass in the month of Nisan, in the twentieth year of King Artaxerxes, *when* wine *was* before him, that I took the wine and gave it to the king. Now I had never been sad in his presence before. ²Therefore the king said to me, "Why *is* your face sad, since you *are* not sick? This *is* nothing but sorrow of heart." So I became dreadfully afraid, ³and said to the king, "May the king live forever! Why should my face not be sad, when the city, the place of my fathers' tombs, *lies* waste, and its gates are burned with fire?" ⁴Then the king said to me, "What do you request?" So I prayed to the God of heaven. ⁵And I said to the king, "If it pleases the king, and if your servant has found favor in your sight, I ask that you send me to Judah, to the city of my fathers' tombs, that I may rebuild it." ⁶Then the king said to me (the queen also sitting beside him), "How long will your journey be? And when will you return?" So it pleased the king to send me; and I set him a time. ⁷Furthermore I said to the king, "If it pleases the king, let letters be given to me for the governors *of the region* beyond the River, that they must permit me to pass through till I come to Judah, ⁸"and a letter to Asaph the keeper of the king's forest, that he must give me timber to make beams for the gates of the citadel which *pertains* to the temple, for the city wall, and for the house that I will occupy." And the king granted *them* to me according to the good hand of my God upon me.

⁹Then I went to the governors *in the region* beyond the River, and gave them the king's letters. Now the king had sent captains of the army and horsemen with me. ¹⁰When Sanballat

the Horonite and Tobiah the Ammonite official heard *of it*, they were deeply disturbed that a man had come to seek the well-being of the children of Israel.

¹¹So I came to Jerusalem and was there three days. ¹²Then I arose in the night, I and a few men with me; I told no one what my God had put in my heart to do at Jerusalem; nor was there any animal with me, except the one on which I rode. ¹³And I went out by night through the Valley Gate to the Serpent Well and the Refuse Gate, and viewed the walls of Jerusalem which were broken down and its gates which were burned with fire. ¹⁴Then I went on to the Fountain Gate and to the King's Pool, but *there was* no room for the animal under me to pass. ¹⁵So I went up in the night by the valley, and viewed the wall; then I turned back and entered by the Valley Gate, and so returned. ¹⁶And the officials did not know where I had gone or what I had done; I had not yet told the Jews, the priests, the nobles, the officials, or the others who did the work.

¹⁷Then I said to them, "You see the distress that we *are* in, how Jerusalem *lies* waste, and its gates are burned with fire. Come and let us build the wall of Jerusalem, that we may no longer be a reproach." ¹⁸And I told them of the hand of my God which had been good upon me, and also of the king's words that he had spoken to me. So they said, "Let us rise up and build." Then they set their hands to *this* good *work*. ¹⁹But when Sanballat the Horonite, Tobiah the Ammonite official, and Geshem the Arab heard *of it*, they laughed at us and despised us, and said, "What *is* this thing that you are doing? Will you rebel against the king?" ²⁰So I answered them, and said to them, "The God of heaven Himself will prosper us; therefore we His servants will arise and build, but you have no heritage or right or memorial in Jerusalem."

Nehemiah 3:1-32

Chapter 3

Rebuilding the Wall

¹Then Eliashib the high priest rose up with his brethren the priests and built the Sheep Gate; they consecrated it and hung its doors. They built as far as the Tower of the Hundred, *and* consecrated it, then as far as the Tower of Hananel. ²Next to *Eliashib* the men of Jericho built. And next to them Zaccur the son of Imri built.

³Also the sons of Hassenaah built the Fish Gate; they laid its beams and hung its doors with its bolts and bars. ⁴And next to them Meremoth the son of Urijah, the son of Koz, made repairs. Next to them Meshullam the son of Berechiah, the son of Meshezabel, made repairs. Next to them Zadok the son of Baana made repairs. ⁵Next to them the Tekoites made repairs; but their nobles did not put their shoulders to the work of their Lord.

⁶Moreover Jehoiada the son of Paseah and Meshullam the son of Besodeiah repaired the Old Gate; they laid its beams and hung its doors, with its bolts and bars. ⁷And next to them Melatiah the Gibeonite, Jadon the Meronothite, the men of Gibeon and Mizpah, repaired the residence of the governor *of the region* beyond the River. ⁸Next to him Uzziel the son of Harhaiah, one of the goldsmiths, made repairs. Also next to him Hananiah, one of the perfumers, made repairs; and they fortified Jerusalem as far as the Broad Wall. ⁹And next to them Rephaiah the son of Hur, leader of half the district of Jerusalem, made repairs. ¹⁰Next to them Jedaiah the son of Harumaph made repairs in front of his house. And next to him Hattush the son of Hashabniah made repairs. ¹¹Malchijah the

son of Harim and Hashub the son of Pahath-Moab repaired another section, as well as the Tower of the Ovens. ¹²And next to him was Shallum the son of Hallohesh, leader of half the district of Jerusalem; he and his daughters made repairs.

¹³Hanun and the inhabitants of Zanoah repaired the Valley Gate. They built it, hung its doors with its bolts and bars, and *repaired* a thousand cubits of the wall as far as the Refuse Gate.

¹⁴Malchijah the son of Rechab, leader of the district of Beth Haccerem, repaired the Refuse Gate; he built it and hung its doors with its bolts and bars.

¹⁵Shallun the son of Col-Hozeh, leader of the district of Mizpah, repaired the Fountain Gate; he built it, covered it, hung its doors with its bolts and bars, and repaired the wall of the Pool of Shelah by the King's Garden, as far as the stairs that go down from the City of David. ¹⁶After him Nehemiah the son of Azbuk, leader of half the district of Beth Zur, made repairs as far as *the place* in front of the tombs of David, to the man-made pool, and as far as the House of the Mighty. ¹⁷After him the Levites, *under* Rehum the son of Bani, made repairs. Next to him Hashabiah, leader of half the district of Keilah, made repairs for his district. ¹⁸After him their brethren, *under* Bavai the son of Henadad, leader of the *other* half of the district of Keilah, made repairs. ¹⁹And next to him Ezer the son of Jeshua, the leader of Mizpah, repaired another section in front of the Ascent to the Armory at the buttress. ²⁰After him Baruch the son of Zabbai carefully repaired the other section, from the buttress to the door of the house of Eliashib the high priest. ²¹After him Meremoth the son of Urijah, the son of Koz, repaired another section, from the door of the house of Eliashib to the end of the house of Eliashib. ²²And after him the priests, the men of the plain, made repairs. ²³After him Benjamin and

Hasshub made repairs opposite their house. After them Azariah the son of Maaseiah, the son of Ananiah, made repairs by his house. [24]After him Binnui the son of Henadad repaired another section, from the house of Azariah to the buttress, even as far as the corner. [25]Palal the son of Uzai *made repairs* opposite the buttress, and on the tower which projects from the king's upper house that *was* by the court of the prison. After him Pedaiah the son of Parosh *made repairs*. [26]Moreover the Nethinim who dwelt in Ophel *made repairs* as far as *the place* in front of the Water Gate toward the east, and on the projecting tower. [27]After them the Tekoites repaired another section, next to the great projecting tower, and as far as the wall of Ophel.

[28]Beyond the Horse Gate the priests made repairs, each in front of his *own* house. [29]After them Zadok the son of Immer made repairs in front of his *own* house. After him Shemaiah the son of Shechaniah, the keeper of the East Gate, made repairs. [30]After him Hananiah the son of Shelemiah, and Hanun, the sixth son of Zalaph, repaired another section. After him Meshullam the son of Berechiah made repairs in front of his dwelling. [31]After him Malchijah, one of the gold-smiths, made repairs as far as the house of the Nethinim and of the merchants, in front of the Miphkad Gate, and as far as the upper room at the corner. [32]And between the upper room at the corner, as far as the Sheep Gate, the goldsmiths and the merchants made repairs.

Nehemiah 4:1-23

Chapter 4

The Wall Defended Against Enemies

¹But it so happened, when Sanballat heard that we were rebuilding the wall, that he was furious and very indignant, and mocked the Jews. ²And he spoke before his brethren and the army of Samaria, and said, "What are these feeble Jews doing? Will they fortify themselves? Will they offer sacrifices? Will they complete it in a day? Will they revive the stones from the heaps of rubbish—*stones* that are burned?" ³Now Tobiah the Ammonite *was* beside him, and he said, "Whatever they build, if even a fox goes up *on it*, he will break down their stone wall."

⁴Hear, O our God, for we are despised; turn their reproach on their own heads, and give them as plunder to a land of captivity! ⁵Do not cover their iniquity, and do not let their sin be blotted out from before You; for they have provoked *You* to anger before the builders.

⁶So we built the wall, and the entire wall was joined together up to half its *height*, for the people had a mind to work.

⁷Now it happened, when Sanballat, Tobiah, the Arabs, the Ammonites, and the Ashdodites heard that the walls of Jerusalem were being restored and the gaps were beginning to be closed, that they became very angry, ⁸and all of them conspired together to come *and* attack Jerusalem and create confusion. ⁹Nevertheless we made our prayer to our God, and because of them we set a watch against them day and night.

¹⁰Then Judah said, "The strength of the laborers is failing, and *there is* so much rubbish that we are not able to build the wall." ¹¹And our adversaries said, "They will neither know nor see anything, till we come into their midst and kill them and

cause the work to cease." [12]So it was, when the Jews who dwelt near them came, that they told us ten times, "From whatever place you turn, *they will be* upon us."

[13]Therefore I positioned *men* behind the lower parts of the wall, at the openings; and I set the people according to their families, with their swords, their spears, and their bows. [14]And I looked, and arose and said to the nobles, to the leaders, and to the rest of the people, "Do not be afraid of them. Remember the Lord, great and awesome, and fight for your brethren, your sons, your daughters, your wives, and your houses."

[15]And it happened, when our enemies heard that it was known to us, and *that* God had brought their plot to nothing, that all of us returned to the wall, everyone to his work. [16]So it was, from that time on, *that* half of my servants worked at construction, while the other half held the spears, the shields, the bows, and *wore* armor; and the leaders *were* behind all the house of Judah. [17]Those who built on the wall, and those who carried burdens, loaded themselves so that with one hand they worked at construction, and with the other held a weapon. [18]Every one of the builders had his sword girded at his side as he built. And the one who sounded the trumpet *was* beside me.

[19]Then I said to the nobles, the rulers, and the rest of the people, "The work *is* great and extensive, and we are separated far from one another on the wall. [20]"Wherever you hear the sound of the trumpet, rally to us there. Our God will fight for us."

[21]So we labored in the work, and half of *the men* held the spears from daybreak until the stars appeared. [22]At the same time I also said to the people, "Let each man and his servant stay at night in Jerusalem, that they may be our guard by night and a working party by day." [23]So neither I, my brethren, my servants, nor the men of the guard who followed me took off our clothes, *except* that everyone took them off for washing.

Nehemiah 5:1-19

Chapter 5

Nehemiah Deals with Oppression

[1]And there was a great outcry of the people and their wives against their Jewish brethren. [2]For there were those who said, "We, our sons, and our daughters *are* many; therefore let us get grain, that we may eat and live." [3]There were also *some* who said, "We have mortgaged our lands and vineyards and houses, that we might buy grain because of the famine." [4]There were also those who said, "We have borrowed money for the king's tax *on* our lands and vineyards. [5]"Yet now our flesh *is* as the flesh of our brethren, our children as their children; and indeed we are forcing our sons and our daughters to be slaves, and *some* of our daughters have been brought into slavery. *It is* not in our power *to redeem them*, for other men have our lands and vineyards."

[6]And I became very angry when I heard their outcry and these words. [7]After serious thought, I rebuked the nobles and rulers, and said to them, "Each of you is exacting usury from his brother." So I called a great assembly against them. [8]And I said to them, "According to our ability we have redeemed our Jewish brethren who were sold to the nations. Now indeed, will you even sell your brethren? Or should they be sold to us?" Then they were silenced and found nothing *to say.* [9]Then I said, "What you are doing *is* not good. Should you not walk in the fear of our God because of the reproach of the nations, our enemies?" [10]"I also, *with* my brethren and my servants, am lending them money and grain. Please, let us stop this usury! [11]"Restore now to them, even this day, their lands, their vineyards, their olive groves, and their houses, also a hundredth

of the money and the grain, the new wine and the oil, that you have charged them." [12]So they said, "We will restore *it*, and will require nothing from them; we will do as you say." Then I called the priests, and required an oath from them that they would do according to this promise. [13]Then I shook out the fold of my garment and said, "So may God shake out each man from his house, and from his property, who does not perform this promise. Even thus may he be shaken out and emptied." And all the assembly said, "Amen!" and praised the LORD. Then the people did according to this promise.

The Generosity of Nehemiah

[14]Moreover, from the time that I was appointed to be their governor in the land of Judah, from the twentieth year until the thirty-second year of King Artaxerxes, twelve years, neither I nor my brothers ate the governor's provisions. [15]But the former governors who *were* before me laid burdens on the people, and took from them bread and wine, besides forty shekels of silver. Yes, even their servants bore rule over the people, but I did not do so, because of the fear of God. [16]Indeed, I also continued the work on this wall, and we did not buy any land. All my servants *were* gathered there for the work. [17]And at my table *were* one hundred and fifty Jews and rulers, besides those who came to us from the nations around us. [18]Now *that* which was prepared daily was one ox *and* six choice sheep. Also fowl were prepared for me, and once every ten days an abundance of all kinds of wine. Yet in spite of this I did not demand the governor's provisions, because the bondage was heavy on this people.

[19]Remember me, my God, for good, *according* to all that I have done for this people.

Nehemiah 6:1-19

Chapter 6

Conspiracy Against Nehemiah

¹Now it happened when Sanballat, Tobiah, Geshem the Arab, and the rest of our enemies heard that I had rebuilt the wall, and *that* there were no breaks left in it (though at that time I had not hung the doors in the gates), ²that Sanballat and Geshem sent to me, saying, "Come, let us meet together among the villages in the plain of Ono." But they thought to do me harm. ³So I sent messengers to them, saying, "I *am* doing a great work, so that I cannot come down. Why should the work cease while I leave it and go down to you?" ⁴But they sent me this message four times, and I answered them in the same manner. ⁵Then Sanballat sent his servant to me as before, the fifth time, with an open letter in his hand. ⁶In it *was* written:

It is reported among the nations, and Geshem says, *that* you and the Jews plan to rebel; therefore, according to these rumors, you are rebuilding the wall, that you may be their king. ⁷And you have also appointed prophets to proclaim concerning you at Jerusalem, saying, '*There is* a king in Judah!' Now these matters will be reported to the king. So come, therefore, and let us consult together.

⁸Then I sent to him, saying, "No such things as you say are being done, but you invent them in your own heart." ⁹For they all *were trying* to make us afraid, saying, "Their hands will be weakened in the work, and it will not be done."

Now therefore, *O God*, strengthen my hands.

¹⁰Afterward I came to the house of Shemaiah the son of

Delaiah, the son of Mehetabel, who *was* a secret informer; and he said, "Let us meet together in the house of God, within the temple, and let us close the doors of the temple, for they are coming to kill you; indeed, at night they will come to kill you." [11]And I said, "Should such a man as I flee? And who *is there* such as I who would go into the temple to save his life? I will not go in!" [12]Then I perceived that God had not sent him at all, but that he pronounced *this* prophecy against me because Tobiah and Sanballat had hired him. [13]For this reason he *was* hired, that I should be afraid and act that way and sin, so *that* they might have *cause* for an evil report, that they might reproach me.

[14]My God, remember Tobiah and Sanballat, according to these their works, and the prophetess Noadiah and the rest of the prophets who would have made me afraid.

[15]So the wall was finished on the twenty-fifth *day* of Elul, in fifty-two days. [16]And it happened, when all our enemies heard *of it*, and all the nations around us saw *these things*, that they were very disheartened in their own eyes; for they perceived that this work was done by our God.

[17]Also in those days the nobles of Judah sent many letters to Tobiah, and *the letters of* Tobiah came to them. [18]For many in Judah were pledged to him, because he was the son-in-law of Shechaniah the son of Arah, and his son Jehohanan had married the daughter of Meshullam the son of Berechiah. [19]Also they reported his good deeds before me, and reported my words to him. Tobiah sent letters to frighten me.

The Holy Bible, New King James Version, (Nashville, Tennessee: Thomas Nelson, Inc.) 1982.